NOT *JUST* A SECRETARY

Using the Job to Get Ahead

Jodie Berlin Morrow & Myrna Lebov

D1572749

A Wiley Press Book

John Wiley & Sons, Inc.

New York • Chichester • Brisbane • Toronto • Singapore

Publisher: Judy V. Wilson
Editor: Betsy Perry
Managing Editor: Katherine Schowalter
Composition and Make-up: The Publisher's Network

Copyright © 1984 by John Wiley & Sons, Inc.

Library of Congress Cataloging in Publication Data

Morrow, Jodie Berlin,
    Not just a secretary.

    Includes index.
    1. Secretaries I. Lebov, Myrna, (co-author) II. Title.
HF5547.5.M67   1983   650,1'4'024651   82-24744
ISBN 0-471-87060-9 (pbk.)

Printed in the United States of America

83 84 10 9 8 7 6 5 4 3 2 1

To Bruce and George, with love

Table of Contents

Acknowledgments

Many people shared their ideas and experiences with us as we were writing this book. Although it is impossible to mention all of these people here, we acknowledge our debt to them. Special thanks go to Georgie Consiglio, Tina LaRusso, Ellen Wilk-Harris, Arnie Castor of Hamilton Systems, Nancy Blakney, Sarah C. Martin, Al Foderaro, Robert Surles, Nancy Marshal, Sally Huns, Mitchell H. Goldstein of Environetics Management Technology, Barbara Rodriguez, Gene Robinson of Telesis, Frank J. Ruck, Jr., Nancy Schneider, Peter Berlin, Bruce Morrow, and George Delury. And finally, our appreciation goes to Joyce Weiss, who gave Jodie her first opportunity, at American Management Associations, to do a career seminar for secretaries, and to Alicia Conklin, whose enthusiasm and valuable editorial suggestions added immeasurably to this book.

Preface

Secretaries are fed up. They are fed up with their low status, with low pay, and with minimal advancement opportunities. It's about time they were fed up, too!

It's time they recognized the full value of their skills. It's time they recognized how much those skills contribute to the success of an organization. And it's time organizations recognized these contributions—and rewarded them not just with pay and respect, but above all, with opportunity for growth.

This book is geared to secretaries who want to get off a dead-end career track. Some of you may want to move to an entirely new occupation, others may want to move ahead within the secretarial field before advancing into management, still others may simply want to move ahead within the secretarial field.

All of you share one thing in common: you want to move. You want to grow. You sense that now is the time to risk asking more from a job. You are right: the time *is* now.

Two new office realities can, if exploited intelligently, enhance your career potential: (1) competent secretaries are in short supply and (2) new, automated office technology offers exciting possibilities for career growth.

Secretaries who have "made it"—who have challenging, satisfying, rewarding jobs either inside the secretarial field or out—have generally found ways to capitalize on the enormous potentials of the secretarial position: being in a key position to learn a lot about the business of an organization, relating to people and assisting them, and coordinating office functions. A secretary is not *just* a secretary. A secretary is a key office staff-member with a wide range of transferable skills. Learning to identify, appreciate, and expand these skills—and getting others to appreciate them—are the crucial steps to maximum career potential.

A fulfilling career *is* within reach. The process is not easy, but it is doable. Many secretaries *have* done it. This book draws on their experiences to tell you how to do it, too.

We know how frustrated many of you are in your jobs. And we know you can do something about it. That's why we wrote this book. When a friend who owns a secretarial agency sponsored a seminar on How Not to Be a Secretary, the response was overwhelming. To an overflow crowd of secretaries, who gave up a Saturday in the heat of a New York summer, Jodie spoke of the basic communication and career-development skills that she herself had to learn, often painfully, during a career switch from schoolteacher to a position as director of training and executive development.

The audience lapped it up. This was information they needed. These were tips they could use to remove the barriers that kept them from achieving their full potential. And these are tips which *you* can use to carve out a fulfilling career.

But this advice is not only for secretaries. In hundreds of other seminars, Jodie has taught secretaries and managers the value of assertiveness and the same ins and outs of career development.

Myrna's background was different from Jodie's. A professional writer and editor, she often had to support herself as a temp in a variety of secretarial and clerical jobs, seeing some of the best and worst of these positions, experiencing both the rewards and frustrations that many of you feel. Now, as editor of a journal that covers the areas of organizational effectiveness and employee development, Myrna knows that the advice offered in this book is necessary for success at any level in an organization.

A word about our gender policy. The book draws on the experience of secretaries, and to date the vast majority have been female—99.1 percent in 1981, according to the Bureau of Labor Statistics. There have been many reports that men are taking secretarial jobs in growing numbers and undoubtedly this is true, especially in a shrinking job market. While our book is geared to *any* secretary who wants to make the most of her or his career, for literary convenience we speak of the secretary as a woman—99.1 percent is an overwhelming figure! The boss is another matter: Managerial ranks are still predominantly male, but since 28% of the positions are now filled by women we feel justified in using him and her interchangeably.

Chapter One

There's Nothing *Wrong* with Being a Secretary

Anne, an executive secretary for a small seminar company, was sitting in her in-laws' living room one Sunday afternoon with her husband's family.

Kathy, her thirteen-year-old niece, was leafing through a book of occupations and salaries.

"Oh, boy!" exclaimed Kathy. "A geologist. Look at what they get! That's what I want to be. No, a doctor! Well, maybe not," she said as her eyes fell on yet another lucrative occupation. "Maybe a systems specialist. That's computers. My teacher says that's where the future lies."

"Oh, I don't know what I want to be," she said as her eyes caught another attractive salary. "Maybe I'll be a secretary until . . ."

"Yuck!" shouted Anne's in-laws, in unison.

"*You* don't want to be a secretary," Kathy's mother said. "You're cut out for much better things. Why with your grades, you should think about being a lawyer."

"That's right, honey," her father agreed. "You can become anything you want!"

Kathy's future safely steered away from secretarial jobs, the family sat back and relaxed.

Except Anne. She was fuming. Silently! Anne was a secretary. "I love my job and I'm good at it," she told herself angrily. "I have a lot of responsibilities and real challenges and a good salary. There's nothing *wrong* with being a secretary. It's what I want to be." But she kept these thoughts to herself.

Consider another typical situation.

Maureen Carlisle makes business decisions, solves problems,

1

resolves interoffice conflicts, talks to customers and suppliers, inputs information to a desk-top computer terminal. She also types letters and transcribes dictation. She is a secretary.

"I've worked for this company for twelve years," she told herself as she read the posted job description of a new opening for assistant sales manager. "It's time to move up." "You can take that notice down now, Maureen," said a voice behind her. It was Bill Green, her boss. "I've just hired someone to fill it. John Dunne. A real go-getter. Just out of college, with a major in marketing."

Maureen left work early that day—with a stomachache.

These are only two of many such incidents which tell the secretary she doesn't get much respect today. Society underrates her job, her boss underrates it, her company underrates it, and yes, *she* underrates it.

What are *your* feelings about the job? Are you satisfied or dissatisfied with the secretarial profession?

You may be just starting out and want to be sure to get on the right track. Perhaps you are a housewife returning to the job market as a secretary and want basic information about the reality of the new business world. Perhaps you are a recent high school or college grad and want to find out how to get the most out of the job.

Or maybe you've been a secretary for some time but only now are experiencing some dissatisfaction with the job. You may have fallen into a secretarial job without thinking; now—maybe years later—you have decided you want another career, one that you have *chosen.* You may have taken a secretarial job with advancement in mind but things are going slowly and you wonder what you're doing wrong. You may feel trapped in what is supposedly an "apprenticeship" job and want to find out how to move. You may have liked being a secretary but now want something different— new challenges, new responsibilities, new rewards offered by a new career.

You may want to remain a secretary but work in a different environment—a doctor or lawyer's office, or the executive offices of a corporate headquarters. You may be trying to decide whether to move ahead within your company or switch to another that offers faster advancement potential. You may want to stay where you are but learn how to cope with the problems of your job. You may want to remain a secretary but get more responsibility and authority.

Or you may be very satisfied with the secretarial profession but want to get new ideas about being a first-rate secretary, keep up with what's going on, get suggestions on personal growth, get reinforcement for what you know is a key role in your company.

How can you get the most out of your job? What do you need to carve out a fulfilling career? How do you change careers? These questions are common to all job holders, especially to genuinely ambitious people. They are basic to anyone's personal and career growth.

We wrote this book because we have experienced many of the same job and career frustrations—problems of communication, self-assertiveness, ambition. We have found answers to many of the questions you are asking about job satisfaction and career advancement, and we're sharing our answers with you. We want to tell you what we have learned, which will help you get ahead in a career.

If we appear to be tough, asking you to take on challenging tasks and to assume much of the responsibility in improving your career, it's because we know that discipline, meeting challenges, and assuming responsibility, both on the job and in your career planning, are necessary to get ahead in the tough business environment. We know that the quickest and surest results will come from your determination and commitment. One Chicago executive told us that secretaries put their own lid on. In this book we're giving you advice on how to take that lid off.

On Anne's first day on the job, she introduced herself to Claire and then asked if she was Bob's secretary.

Claire replied no. "I'm an assistant program director," she said.

Anne soon learned that Claire was both, although she resented being referred to, and used, as a secretary. If someone asked her to type a label, and that task was not part of her work for Bob, she had a quick response: "No, that's not my job."

In a small office, where employee teamwork was vital, Claire was a bottleneck. She also created resentment among the other secretaries who were willing to help Claire in a pinch but could not count on her to reciprocate.

A high school graduate with no college credits behind her and two years on the job, Claire felt she deserved to be promoted to program director. She did take one step toward career advancement—communicating her career objective to her boss and others in the company—but she failed to take other key steps.

What are these other steps?

• Have an in-depth career planning talk with a boss. Claire failed to talk with her boss to determine whether she *could* advance to program director at the company, and if so, what she could do to prepare for that move. Her key step would be to find out what she needed to do to move on.

• Get additional education. Claire did not want to spend the time or take the trouble to go to college. She refused to enroll in a degree program and balked at taking individual courses as well. However, she needed to fill gaps in her knowledge in order to function effectively in the position she thought was due her.

• Do job-related research. She failed to read up on or do other practical research in her company's field.

• Offer suggestions for programs or policies. Claire didn't come up with ideas that showed the independent judgment, creativity, and follow-through necessary to plan a program. In other words, she showed no sign of capability for the job she wanted.

Claire took none of these steps. Instead, she seethed with resentment that her company offered no opportunity for advancement.

"I just have no luck," Claire complained to Anne with increasing regularity. "I'm just stuck in a dead-end secretarial job."

We don't agree. It's not simply luck that lands you in the job you want. Commitment is the key. Commitment to your objectives, to your on-the-job effectiveness, to your growth, to yourself. In a very real sense, you produce your own opportunities.

You must be committed to finding out what you want to do, what you are skilled to do, what you can do to achieve your objectives. In other words, the path of commitment takes knowledge about yourself, your capabilities, your interests and values, and the possibilities open to you through your own efforts and through the efforts of others. Career development doesn't just happen. You make it happen—but not overnight! A lot of work is required to make it happen.

We're big on commitment in this book and on what you can do to make things happen. Commitment is the key to shaping your career and to taking control of your life. But we're not blinding ourselves to the realities of your work world. We know many of the problems you face as a secretary. Most companies structure the secretary's job as a ghetto. There are no established career paths, and it's difficult to forge your own. But our book will give you advice on how to break out of the ghetto, how to identify and appreciate your skills, how to clarify your job-related values, how to make a career decision, and how to work toward your career objective.

Sometimes you simply need to know that you *can* move ahead. Many women don't know this because they have been taught to apply their own "internal brakes" to a fast-moving career. Traditionally, secretaries have viewed their career, if they considered it at all, as subordinate to their job, rather than the job as part of a career. This attitude must change if secretaries are to develop challenging and rewarding careers in which a series of responsibilities leads to other responsibilities and to a career of growth and professional self-fulfillment. Often just thinking in terms of a career instead of a job is a major breakthrough; and taking an active role in achieving it may seem "pushy." But what seems pushy at first may very quickly come to be seen as the natural and necessary steps that will enable you to make things happen in your career.

And what about those of you who want to remain a secretary? You, too, want to make things happen. Perhaps you want to find a more challenging secretarial job or a more appreciative boss or a job in a growth industry. Or perhaps you want to feel better about choosing to be a secretary. Remember the reaction of Anne's family to the possibility that young Kathy might want to be a secretary, even for a short time? There's a lot of social pressure today *not* to be a secretary, especially if you are intelligent and competent. The women's movement, by encouraging women to aim high and by fighting the discrimination that holds them back, has also fed the idea that a secretarial position is demeaning.

We're not saying that you should or should not be a secretary, but we are saying that you need to look carefully at what you have done, can do, and want to do, and then get the best job possible in line with *your* objectives. A secretarial job might fit your needs perfectly. Anne would have achieved a major breakthrough if she had announced confidently to her family that "I am a secretary and I am proud of it." For Anne was a secretary by choice at that stage in her career. She liked the variety in her job, she liked her boss, she knew her boss respected her abilities, she received a very good salary, she was at the decision-making center in her company; yet she had no desire to make policy herself or to determine profit-making strategies. Anne's job did enable her to make things happen in her company! She knew it but couldn't affirm it to others. Our book will help you better appreciate the importance of the secretarial job. And it will point to ways that you can enrich it further, either by expanding your current job or by finding a new position that will provide you with the professional self-fulfillment you seek.

A SELLER'S MARKET

The times are ripe for things to happen. The 1980s offer unparalleled job-market opportunities to the secretary. Never before has the need for competent secretaries been so great, and never before have so many openings gone unfilled. In 1980, the Bureau of Labor Statistics reports, there were 3,876,000 secretaries and stenographers in the U.S., with over 300,000 unfilled openings. Recent government projections indicate this field will continue to be one of the fastest growing in the U.S.: by 1990, there are expected to be 5,357,000 secretaries.

What does this optimistic job picture boil down to? Simple. Secretaries will be in demand. It's a seller's market, and secretaries are in the enviable position of being able to choose to whom they will sell their services. It's time to use your smarts and choose the secretarial opening that can help you move toward the career objectives *you* choose.

A whole new set of tools is at your disposal. Secretaries who can use the new automated equipment efficiently and creatively are those most in demand. You can help companies realize the promise of increased productivity offered by office automation. But you must seize the initiative if you want to use that equipment as tools in your career advancement strategy. Automation is a double-edged sword for the secretary: it can help you do your routine tasks faster and more efficiently and free up your time for the more challenging, career-enhancing responsibilities. Or, it can allow you to accomplish routine tasks in less time and simply make you available for more of the same.

Figure out how office automation can help you advance in your career. Do you want to work for a manufacturer and vendor of the equipment? Or do you want to work for an organization that uses the equipment? In what capacity do you want to work? The task now is to find out where and how you want to fit in and then work toward your goals. Office automation offers wide-open opportunities. Make those opportunities work for you and your career. You can do it.

KEY CONCEPTS

You need to develop the best techniques to land a job that will be the start of a career, to find the right boss, assert yourself with that boss, and to project a promotable image. The key concepts in understanding those techniques are:

Self-enhancement. Secretaries must avoid self-defeating behavior and adopt self-enhancing ways of thinking and acting.

Confidence is vital. The Chicago executive who told us that "secretaries put their own lid on" also said that what holds them back is their view of what the secretary does. They see the secretary as a "super go-fer." They do not make use of the vast potential of the position and thus do not carve out a challenging and rewarding job. They lack the confidence to take the risks necessary for moving ahead.

Career objectives. Defining a career objective gives the secretary a direction to head in. Failure to choose an objective condemns her to an overwhelming sea of options and generally keeps her "in her place." An objective based on identified skills, however, takes the secretary out of the realm of the 'wouldn't-it-be-nice-if-I-could' fantasy and places her firmly in the real world, where possibilities are achievable.

Strategic job-placement. Locating the career-building job and a supportive boss are vital to a secretary's career growth. There are clues to look for and action to take. Chapters 9 through 13 provide tips on what you need to know and do.

Skills. All skills are useful and many are necessary, but some are more important than others in terms of career enhancement. Decision-making and problem-solving skills are highly regarded, especially when a manager uses them; typing is not, especially when a secretary does it.

Organizations are changing and the categories of skills are broadening. Current management theory favors a switch from a traditional authoritarian approach, in which the boss does all the thinking and gives the orders, to a more participative environment, in which the employees make the decisions and solve problems in their work areas.

Organizations *say* they want to use an employee's full potential, and secretaries *say* they can contribute more to an organization. Obviously the time is right for the secretary to use the new management theory to her advantage—and the company's.

The time is also right for you to recognize the full range of a secretary's skills: she does make decisions, she does solve problems, she does deal with people, she does communicate verbally and in writing. These and many others are "secretarial skills" just as much as typing and filing are. It's up to you to expand these skills and use them to enrich your career or, if you choose, to transfer them to another profession. It's up to you to take the risks necessary to move ahead.

And it's up to you to see yourself as more than *just* a secretary.

Chapter Two

More Than Typing and Steno

Is the following scene familiar?

A close friend from high school bumps into you in the street. Shrieks of recognition follow. You haven't seen each other for ten years.

"What are you doing now?" she asks.

"Oh, I'm just a secretary," you answer.

"Ahhh," she says.

You separate a short time later, vowing to keep in touch. But somehow, you feel your chance encounter has been ruined. What's eating at you? What's wrong?

You mull over the conversation, word for word. "Oh, I'm just a secretary," echoes in your mind. "Just a secretary. Just."

"Dammit," you exclaim aloud, "I run the office. I work my butt off! Why did I say *just* a secretary?

A good question!

SELF-APPRECIATION, JOB-APPRECIATION

If the response in the preceding story strikes a familiar chord, if you speak of yourself as *"just* a secretary," you have a lot of work ahead. You have to reexamine what you do in your secretarial job and what you want to do. You might decide that you want to stay within the secretarial profession but itch for more recognition and more appreciation. Or you might decide that while it may be a pretty important job and your boss appreciates your hard work, *you* don't! Or you might decide that you're fed up with being *"just* a secretary," and are ready to more on!

Consider this situation.

June is a fifty-four-year-old secretary in the employee relations department of a large chemical company. If you asked her two months ago what she did, she, too, would have answered, "just a secretary." Today, she says that she is responsible for benefits administrations for 4,800 employees. Her responsibilites: finding forms; tracking down information about benefits, pension plans, vacation time, and coverage dates; communicating the information to employees and their families; and maintaining company records. Her on-the-job skills: research, compilation and evaluation of information, clear communication, and public relations. After doing the exercises that we recommend later in this chapter, she found she used precisely the skills she would have in her fantasy job: archaeologist. She was in the right job! She didn't have to moon about not being an archaeologist, an unrealistic career objective for a fifty-four-year-old secretary without a college degree. Her objective became growth in her current position.

As with June, the first step in appreciating yourself on the job is to understand *exactly* what you do. A statement like, "Oh I'm just a secretary," is a blanket dismissal of your worth. And if you casually dismiss the importance of your job and your expertise at it, why shouldn't others do so, too?

What you need are details. Lots of them. Details about what tasks you perform; how much time you devote to them per day, per week, per month; and what skills are involved in each task. Finally you must understand how your job—and you—help make your organization operate effectively. What credit can you claim for your organization's success?

For example: say you are secretary to the president of a dress manufacturing company. One of your responsibilities is to determine which phone calls your boss should take personally, which should be passed down to lower-level employees, which you can handle yourself, and which are really not for anyone in your organization. If the call is from a young, unknown designer, it may be worth a lot to your company, or it may be worth nothing at all. You can be sure that an executive who took the call would recognize what it was worth—and would claim credit for it if it led to profits. The skills used during that brief phone conversation include communication, public relations, evaluation of information, knowledge of the organizational structure and staffing, referral, and decision-making. Typing and steno are not the secretary's sole reasons for being; in fact, today they are not even the primary reasons.

WHAT IS A SKILL?

A skill is an ability you have that's useful to others. It may be a natural ability or one that you worked hard to develop. What's important is that you can use it to perform a task essential to your job. But it's not limited to use in your current job. A skill can be applied to tasks basic to other jobs, perhaps to jobs at a considerably higher level of responsibility and creativity than your current one.

Richard Bolles, author of *What Color Is Your Parachute?*, a very useful guide for job hunters and career changers, refers to skills as "building blocks," and that's exactly what they are. They are a collection of learned or innate abilities that can be arranged and rearranged in a variety of patterns, to apply in a variety of jobs.

Consider the example of Karen.

Karen was a secretary for eight years, she worked for the president of a major magazine, and for a United States senator. Today she sells ads for a magazine. She is very successful at sales, and she loves it. She was also very successful at her secretarial jobs, but she hated them. While a secretary, she never saw much value in her job—or in herself—but now she sees she developed skills as a secretary which contribute to her success in sales today. Those skills? Assured telephone presence, conveying essential information succinctly and persuasively, public relations, evaluation of information, clear writing, decision-making, problem-solving, and dealing with people. In short, her sales job requires effective communication skills, and she strengthened those skills in her hated secretarial jobs.

"Maybe it wasn't so bad after all," Karen admits now. "I learned a lot on the job. I picked up a lot of important knowledge about publishing at the magazine, and I certainly had to learn how to handle people when I worked for the senator. I wouldn't be such a good sales person now if I hadn't been such a good secretary before."

It is important to remember that a skill need not be learned on the job in order to apply it to the job setting. It may be something you learned as a hobby or as part of your family responsibilities. For example, a working mother frequently juggles people and tasks, coordinating schedules for herself, her children, and her husband. Who shops for the week's food? When? Who cooks? Who does the dishes? Who cleans house? How does she arrange that all the morning tasks at home get done in time for everyone to get where they˙ need to be? The mother-wife is a coordinator—and she'd better be efficient or there will be a lot of uneven tempers around the house.

Coordination is a major business skill and it can be applied in any number of jobs. It certainly is necessary for the secretarial job, but it's also vital for office managers, conference programmers, TV producers, assistant TV producers, PR consultants, sales persons, sales managers, advertising account excutives, and many, many others.

Transferability

To gain an appreciation of what you do, and acquire confidence in what you *can* do, you must know in detail what your job entails. What you do now, or what you have done, translates into skills. These skills can be transferred to either an expanded secretarial position or to another type of job. These skills are your building blocks, and you are going to arrange them into a new pattern that will either take you out of your secretarial job or enhance it.

Your first step is to be aware of the full range of skills that go into being "*just* a secretary." Then you will identify those skills which *you* use as a secretary. And finally you will transfer these skills to a new career objective for yourself. We'll say more about career objectives in chapters 10 and 11.

WHAT ARE THE SECRETARY'S SKILLS?

Ask a nonsecretary what are the secretary's main skills and the answer will probably be typing and steno. Ask a secretary the same question, and unfortunately, she may give the same answer. In fact Arnie, a friend of ours who runs a successful secretarial employment agency, who has great respect for the secretary's abilities, and who is dead certain that a secretary can use her job to get ahead, also identified the secretary's skills as typing and steno!

When we suggested that secretarial skills might also include effective communication, public relations, organization, coordination, planning, time management, problem-solving, and decision-making, he was at first confused. "But we're talking of mechanical skills—typing and steno and operating word processors. *Those* are secretarial skills!" he insisted.

Yes, they are. But so are a host of other secretarial functions that are associated more with managers and executives than with secretaries. And effective secretaries can parlay them into a higher-level job. But first let's talk about those "mechanical" skills.

Typing, Steno, Word Processing. Typing and steno are a secretary's bread-and-butter skills. They should not be undervalued. First of all, they are *measurable,* and that makes it easier for a potential employer to determine an applicant's skill in this area. If decision-making could be measured in terms of quantity and quality (Just think of timing a potential vice president of marketing on the number of decisions made without error in five minutes!) rest assured that it would be. But it can't, and typing and steno can.

So, typing and steno are generally the keys to getting the secretary her job, and the more skilled you are in them, the likelier it is you will get your foot in the door of a career-positioning job. If you use them intelligently, they will reward you well. But always remember that these are only two of your many skills.

Not only will typing and steno help you land your career-positioning job, but these are also handy skills to take with you as you climb the career ladder. This is especially true today—and it will be increasingly important in the future when the vice-president of marketing will have a desktop computer terminal and she'll use her typing skills to enter and retrieve the information that will help her make decisions. Tomorrow's would-be executives who hold that typing is "beneath" them are likely to find themselves blocked from higher-level jobs that will depend on exciting new office technology. (We'll discuss more about the office of the future and the secretary's role in it in chapter 14.)

In fact, you may well be at an advantage! Without any highfalutin resistance to the keyboard, you will be ready to function more effectively than a would-be manager entrenched in the idea that typing is only for secretaries.

Dealing with People. As a secretary, you interact with many individuals at many levels of authority and responsibility. You have to do this so regularly, in fact, that you and others might not even be aware of the skill involved. A secretary can offend, she can placate, she can inspire trust, she can sell, she can antagonize, she can anger, she can tease, she can amuse—in short, she deals with people. And, to be successful for yourself and your organization, you constantly must deal with people in an effective and efficient manner.

Don't underestimate the importance of "people-skills" for yourself and for your organization. A mark of a successful manager and executive is the ability to motivate and lead other people—and that, too, is the mark of a secretary destined to move up the career ladder.

Public Relations. Related to people-skills is the secretary's ability to promote herself and her organization with people on the outside. You have frequent contact with outsiders: you are often on the phone with them, you greet visitors, and you channel them to the right people. In fact, you are often the one who initially establishes the favorable relationship between your organization and individuals outside of it. And that's PR, a very sought-after and highly paid skill in today's society.

Communication. To deal effectively with people, which we've just set as one of the most important secretarial skills, you must be able to get the message across. You must be able to express yourself so as to avoid misunderstanding, bruised feelings, and other negative reactions. Tact and tenacity are the earmarks of good communication skills.

Speaking plainly and clearly is the most effective means of getting the message across. And the same goes for written communication. It's crucial to learn how to write a persuasive memo (see chapter 7). If you show skill in your written communciations, you may be given authority to draft some of the correspondence for your boss. And eventually for yourself.

Handling Information. Reams of information that require constant judgments pass over the secretary's desk. She must collect the information, organize it, sift it, decide what gets priority, and channel it to the right persons. Lack of skill in this area can be disastrous for your boss and for your organization, since vital information can get lost by a disorganized or distracted secretary.

Information is organized for future referral through a filing system, perhaps the most hated of all secretarial responsibilities and, in the eyes of many, the most mindless. Not so! Filing systems can range from simple to elaborate. The organization and maintenance of an easily accessible and understandable filing system requires the ability to think clearly, consistently, and logically so you and others can get the information you need, when you need it. These skills are among the rarest and most valuable in any corporation.

Information is power, and the secretary who acts as a clearing house for information wields a potentially potent tool. We're not saying that information should be brandished as a weapon—discretion in deciding what information should be passed on, and to whom, is the key—but the intelligent handling of it gives a secretary more power than she might be aware of.

Coordination. The secretary is not a circus performer—although sometimes your office may *seem* like a circus. A competent secretary must be a ringmaster, or at least an adept juggler of time, people, tasks, and money. Maintaining a schedule—yours and your boss's—is a valuable skill that should not be underestimated. In the higher reaches of the organization, coordination of time and tasks is known as time management, coordination of money is known as financial management, and coordination of personnel is known as human resources management, and they're reflected in fancy organization charts. Coordination, in short, is an integral function of management and you, as a secretary, have already practiced it extensively.

Hand in hand with coordination go the skills of planning and setting priorities. Secretaries, especially when they're starting, often work for a couple of people. Organizing a work load and determining priorities are essential. As one secretary told us, "If you can't figure out how to organize in order to get the most important things done on time, you're not going to make it as a secretary." And you certainly won't make it in higher-level positions either.

Finance and Accounting Fundamentals. No, you are not required to draft a company budget, but it may well be your responsibility to assemble and organize the data on which the budget is based. Secretaries often assist their bosses in routine financial tasks, and this requires familiarity with basic business and accounting principles. Working with your boss, you also pick up knowledge of your organization's financial goals. Along the way, you may even learn to read a balance sheet. Moving up the career ladder will give you frequent opportunity to draw on your knowledge of bottom-line financial reality, learned in your secretarial position.

Problem Solving. Effective leaders in any organization are effective problem solvers. But today, management theory recognizes that problem-solving skills are not the province of only managers or executives. In fact, if problems do get solved, quite often the effective solutions are proposed lower down the line, and certainly they are carried out there. High-level management often is not close enough to the problem to know what to do about it.

The secretary is close—too close, it may seem—to problems in the office, and often she can propose and carry out the most effective solutions. The process she goes through is the same one high-level managers go through: perception of a problem, research and analysis of the causes, suggestion of alternative solutions, selection of the best solution, and follow-up.

Experience and initiative in problem-solving at lower levels of the organization boosts the standing of the employee and marks that individual for potential promotion. You must be alert to the fact that passivity toward and tolerance of problems will chain you to a lower-level, less responsible position. You must actively look for and suggest solutions to problems if you want to move up the ladder of success.

Decision-Making. Decision-making and problem-solving are the two major activities associated with effective managers. One president of a Chicago company told us not long ago that his ̍ decision-making skills were a major reason for his success. And part of the secret of his decision-making talents was to allow—and in fact require—his staff to make as many decisions as possible.

The decisions that a secretary makes and those that the Chicago executive makes are very different—but only in degree. The executive will make the strategic decisions which determine the course of the organization overall, while the secretary will make decisions that determine how efficient and effective her and her boss's areas within the organization are.

Although the decisions may be different in degree, the process is nevertheless the same. You, like the executive, must weigh options, choose one on the basis of good judgment, and sell the decision to others. Don't forget that, while the executive has the power to make the decision, he must sell it to those who will carry it out. Similarly, you will have to sell your decision to your boss.

Office Procedures.   Offices don't run smoothly on their own. Find an efficiently run office, and behind it you will find efficient office procedures. And behind those procedures you will likely find a secretary or administrative assistant who carries them out or even sets them up. Being closest to the action, the secretary is often the one who can make realistic suggestions for change. This is an area where you most certainly draw on problem-solving skills, since any change is usually a problem and office snafus are often the stickiest.

HOW TO CREATE *YOUR* SKILLS INVENTORY

Now for a personal confession: the rundown of secretarial skills in the preceding section was supposed to be very brief, perhaps only a couple of paragraphs. We despaired as the list of skills grew and grew. And, more than likely, you can think of even more skills that you have acquired on the job—let alone off!

So let's now identify *your* skills. We shall limit our examination to an inventory of skills used on the job, but the same approach can be applied to skills you use off the job, and to skills for a new or expanded position.

The goal of a skills inventory is to pin down precisely what tasks you perform and what skills are involved in those tasks. When you first begin, you probably will be vague. But as you concentrate on the analysis, you will become more specific. Your understanding and appreciation of your skills will snowball. If this doesn't happen, it might mean that you need to develop more skills.

Try to be particularly sensitive to skills needed in jobs that you might want to aim for. If you don't know what career you want, though, that's OK. Discovering what skills you use will probably help you realize that you prefer using some to others, and that realization may suggest what sort of career you want. You may even find you are using some of the very skills required in your desired career.

Free Association

Doing an inventory of your skills demands absolute concentration and, at the same time, creative free association.

By free association, we mean letting your mind wander. It allows your deepest and, perhaps, hidden thoughts to float to the surface. With free association, you get out of the traditional thought patterns that may have bogged you down in a secretarial rut. For example, suppose you note in your skills inventory that you spent over three hours that day working on the staff's time cards, double-checking the figures and transferring them to time sheets. What a bore! your mind tells you. No wonder you hate this job.

"I hate figures!" you tell yourself. "But wasn't it fun when I discovered Jim's figures didn't add up? I sure liked the admiration in his eyes when I showed him. And I'm not bad with figures. I actually *like* balancing my checkbook down to the last penny. If I'm off by a few dollars, I'll stick with it until I find the error. In fact, I *like* tracking down the mistake. Jim even called me 'Sherlock Holmes' when I showed him that error. I do hate figures, but I guess I like to solve problems. I want to be challenged, not made to feel like a dull recording machine."

So, where does this free association lead? To the possibility that you enjoy working with figures, that you're good at it, that you are careful with them, that you persevere until you balance your accounts. What you hate is the dull routine work with figures. But you hate the other routine aspects of your job, too. These are important insights. You must keep them in mind as you track down the correct job for you.

The lesson? Both creative free association and absolute concentration are necessary for a successful skills inventory, which is essential for creative career positioning.

Time Log

We have already spelled out activities that secretaries often perform. You probably perform some of these, or all of them. Or you may perform others. Good! Our listing of secretarial activities and skills is a composite rundown. We cannot tailor it to your specific achievements. That's for you to do with a time log.

A time log is a record of performance. It is the best way to know exactly what you do, and when. While it's easy to describe how to keep a time log, it is not as easy to do one. It takes time—though not an impossible amount. It takes attention—you must remember to record your activities. And it takes persistence. You might catch yourself saying, "Oh, I'm too busy to record that now. I'll remember it at the end of the day." Believe us, you won't! The time to record your activities is at the very time you perform them.

There are many ways to do a time log. Some of them might seem less time-consuming than the way we suggest. Why not take advantage of shortcuts? Because we have found that shortcuts in time logs shortchange you. Some experts supply you with a form with the hours (or half hours or quarter hours) printed on it, asking you simply to fill in your activities in the appropriate time slot. This type of form will not work for you—your day is likely to be too fragmented to fit comfortably into those time slots. At the end of the first two hours, you are very likely to throw up your hands in disgust.

Your time log is tailor-made by you. No fancy forms, no standard time slots.

The best—and simplest—way to keep an accurate time log is to jot down when you begin an activity and when you end it. Every activity! Make your notations as brief as possible, but supply enough detail so you can analyze the activity at the end of the day.

Say you are June, the benefits assistant described earlier in the chapter. Your time log might look like our sample. Your call to an insurance company should be recorded like this:

4:15   phone, me/ins. co. (Ross)   4:30

This is easy to decipher. You placed the call at 4:15 and finished it at 4:30. The topic was R. Ross, the beneficiary of an employee who had died six months earlier. If the call was *from* the insurance company, simply record:

4:15   phone, ins. co./me (Ross)   4:30

An entry for drafting and typing a memo might read:

3:00   memo/staff (blood drive)   3:30

᛫ Note the name of the person or group to whom the memo is addressed (or to whom the call is made) and specify the subject. If you

SAMPLE TIME LOG

8:30	Check mail & route it	8:45
8:45	Get coffee for Brown & me	9:00
9:00	Phone, Cane/me (disability info.)	9:05
9:05	Phone Shield/me (med. benefits quest.)	9:10
9:10	Instruct Cohen on pension forms	9:15
9:15	Ans. phone for Brown	9:15
9:15	Check files for Shield	9:20
9:20	Phone, me/ins. co. (Shield)	9:30
9:30	Ans. phone for Brown	9:30
9:30	Org. vacation benefits info. for Brown's mtg.	9:50
9:50	Sharpen pencils, chat	10:00
10:00	Benefits orientation for new employees (10:00 ans. phone for Brown 10:00)	10:45
10:50	Met with Brown re govt. forms	11:05
11:05	Type accident log rpt. (11:10 ans. phone for Brown 11:10)	11:20
11:20	Type forms for new employees (11:35 phone, Abrams/me—vac. benefits 11:40)	12:00
12:00	Lunch	1:15
1:15	Mtg., Jones (disability claims)	1:35
1:35	Steno, Brown (correspondence)	2:00
2:00	Type corr. (2:10 ans. phone for Brown 2:10) (2:15 phone, Smith/me—vac. benefits info. 2:20)	2:30
2:30	Xerox all new forms, chat	3:00
3:00	Draft memo/staff (blood drive) (3:15 file search/rpt. on '81 drive 3:20)	3:30
3:30	Mtg., Ross (beneficiary of emp. who died 6 mos. ago; still awaiting check)	4:15
4:15	Phone, me/ins. co. (info. on Ross check)	4:30
4:30	File all forms for new employees	4:55
5:00	Leave	

perform a related task as part of the overall activity, note that on the line after the main activity. For example, in parentheses you might record (3:15 file search/rpt. on '81 drive 3:20) to remind you of the research skills used in drafting the memo. Also put in parentheses any brief interruptions.

Remember: be specific, be persistent, be complete. Record, record, record. If you find the task tedious, remember that it is the only way to get the details on how you spend the day. Keep in mind the benefits to *you*, and the drawbacks will fade quickly. After all, you might find that filing a week's correspondence is boring, yet you do it because it's part of your job. Well, keeping a detailed time log is part of the job of identifying your job skills—and you will be the beneficiary.

Skills Inventory

Save time at the end of each day to analyze your time log. Do it either at the office or at home, but do it! The time log, without the analysis, will be a waste of time.

On a separate sheet of paper, write out the skills involved in each of the activities cited in your time log. For example, the memo to the staff required writing, editing, and proofreading. These are editorial skills. Your call to the insurance company? Wasn't it to get information? Isn't that a research skill? Didn't many of your activities involve people? Didn't you use interpersonal skills to deal with nervous, angry, grieving, impatient people (employees, beneficiaries, relatives of employees); with the insurance company; with your boss? Didn't these interactions require a wide range of communication skills?

After you complete this breakdown, estimate the amount of time spent during the day on each skill—this is part one of your skills inventory. At the end of a week, add up the time spent on each skill—and that becomes part two of your skills inventory. Do the inventory carefully. It is your key in choosing a realistic career objective. (More on that in chapters 10 and 11.)

SAMPLE SKILLS INVENTORY (Part I)

Time Log Slot	Skills	Time Spent
8:30-8:45	Information organization & analysis	15 min.
9:00-9:05	Communication (phone)	5
,,	Policy interpretation	5
9:05-9:10	Communication (phone)	5
9:10-9:15	Instruction (mtg)	5
9:15-9:20	Research (files)	5
9:20-9:30	Research (phone)	10
,,	Intercompany liaison	10

SAMPLE SKILLS INVENTORY (Part I) (continued)

Time Log Slot	Skills	Time Spent
9:05-9:30		
(minus 9:10-9:15)	Problem solving (for emp. Shield—see 9:05)	20 min.
9:30-9:50	Information organization	20
10:00-10:45	Instruction (mtg)	45
10:50-11:05	Policy coordination & clarification	15
,,	Communication (mtg)	15
11:05-11:20	Information organization	10
,,	Typing	10
,,	Proofreading	5
11:20-12:00	Typing	25
,,	Proofreading	10
(11:35-11:40)	Communication (phone)	5
,,	Policy interpretation	5
1:15-1:35	Communication (mtg)	20
,,	Policy interpretation	15
,,	Computation	5
,,	Tact	20
,,	Problem solving	20
1:35-2:00	Steno	25
2:00-2:30	Typing, layout	10
,,	Grammar, spelling	5
,,	Rewriting	5
,,	Proofreading	5
,,	Research (files)	5
(2:15-2:20)	Communication (phone)	5
,,	Policy interpretation	5
3:00-3:30	Promotion	30
,,	Planning	15
,,	Decision making	10
,,	Communication written	15
(3:15-3:20)	Research (files)	5

Time Log		Time
Slot	Skills	Spent
3:30-4:15	Public relations	45 min.
,,	Tact	45
,,	Communication (mtg)	45
4:15-4:30	Communication (phone)	15
3:30-4:30 (inclusive)	Intercompany liaison	15
,,	Research (mtg & phone)	60
,,	Problem solving	60
,,	Decision making	60
4:30-4:55	Information organization	25

SAMPLE SKILLS INVENTORY (Part I) (continued)

As you can see, even a "simple" task like typing a letter involves a wide range of skills. Of course in situations where you draft the letter, the skills are multiplied. That is why, if you add up the time spent on your various skills, the total is greater than the number of hours in your work day.

Remember, it is very important to work on your skills inventory at the end of each day. You don't want to forget exactly what went into that phone call to the insurance company.

At the end of a week, you will have a fairly complete picture of your skills. A month later, you might want to do another time log and skills inventory as a check. You might be involved in other tasks that require other skills. Moreover, you will be familiar with the process of doing the log, and you might be more sensitive to the skills.

There is no better way for a secretary to acquire an appreciation of her worth than for her to detail exactly what she does and to translate these tasks into skills that can be used in other jobs as well.

Fantasize About Your Ideal Job

After you complete the time log and skills inventory—and recuperate from the rigorous analysis that went into them—try another exercise, one in transferability.

What is your ideal job? Forget about whether you are qualified for such a job. Forget about whether it is a realistic career objective. Fantasize. Assume that you are qualified, and that the job is realistic. The job is yours. Now, what does it entail?

Imagine a day on your ideal job. What are the activities? Be as detailed as possible. Don't block out those enticing perks that you

SAMPLE SKILLS INVENTORY (Part 2 Composite Time)	
Skills	**Time**
Information organization & analysis	70 min.
Communication (phone)	35
Communication (meetings)	80
Communication (written)	15
Policy interpretation	30
Instruction	50
Research (files)	15
Research (phone)	25
Research (meetings)	45
Intercompany liaison	25
Problem-solving	100
Decision-making	70
Typing	45
Steno	25
Computation	5
Grammar & spelling	5
Proofreading	20
Planning	15
Promotion	30
Public relations	45
Tact	65
Policy coordination & clarification	15

are certain are part of your ideal job but seem totally absent from your present one.

As with your skills inventory, analyze the skills required for each of the tasks involved in your ideal job. Stop and think. Is there anything in your current job that resembles that task or requires that skill? Are you really doing that task now, or something very much like it, but downplaying it because it's "just" part of your secretarial job? Can you appreciate those skills if used in your ideal job but not if used in your current job? If so, why? Can you begin to make the connection between the skills used on your current job and those required for your ideal job?

Remember, your skills are your building blocks, and you can rearrange them into new and interesting and challenging jobs. Perhaps you can even arrange them into your ideal job.

Chapter Three

Projecting a Professional Image

Sarah, an executive secretary, had been working until 9 P.M. two or three nights a week for almost a year. Her boss was a workaholic and she was forced to become one, too, just to keep up with the steady stream of memos, correspondence, and proposals.

"I've asked my boss for an assistant," Sarah told participants of an assertive communication seminar, "and I even sent a memo. She said she was "working on it'."

"How did you ask for an assistant, Sarah?" one seminar participant asked.

"I said, 'I *must* have an assistant! I can't handle this work load alone'."

"Were you smiling when you made the request? You are now."

Sarah looked confused. "Am I?" she asked. "But I'm serious about this. I was serious when I made the request. At least, I *meant* to be serious!"

Suddenly all the seminar participants—including Sarah—became aware that Sarah smiled constantly. She didn't look as if she meant what she said, unless of course she meant to be joking. In short, she was sending a double message.

The next week Sarah returned to the seminar triumphant. She had made her pitch to her boss again, this time without smiling. Because now her body language matched her verbal language, her boss took her seriously. She would get an assistant the next week. And that was something to smile about!

Sarah's problem—being taken seriously—is one of a secretary's most common problems. It may be one of yours. Do you mean to be serious but don't get taken seriously? If the answer is yes, you may have an image problem.

What Is an Image?

Very simply, an image is the projection of your character and your style. It's the impression you make on other people.

We hear the word *image* a lot today. Not long ago President Reagan's advisors were worried about Mrs. Reagan's "image problem." In a time of growing unemployment and hard economic times, her taste for expensive clothes, ritzy parties, and high living—in short, her image—stirred resentment among the public; and such resentment is a political liability.

Efforts were soon underway to change Nancy Reagan's image. Interviews and articles began to project the image of a sincere, caring woman who was deeply devoted to her husband and to the country.

The tools at your disposal are different from those of Nancy Reagan, but you can be just as effective, maybe more so, in changing your image.

The Right Image. A successful image is based on underlying realities—seriousness about your career, belief in your skills, and a firm commitment to your objectives. Once you inventory your skills, identify your job interests, and begin your career planning, you are on your way to developing commitment to your career growth. And commitment generates energy, perhaps the foremost determinant of image.

"Well sure, energy is fine," you might be saying at this point. "Just tell me how to get it. From pills? From eight hours of sleep a night? What about a good solid pep-talk from the boss?"

No, none of the above.

Image-feeding energy is both a by-product and a generator. It stems from confidence, which is a by-product of self-knowledge, self-acceptance, and assertive self-definition—belief in oneself and one's demonstrated abilities, and commitment to personal objectives.

As a generator, energy breeds more achievement, greater satisfaction, stronger belief in your ability to do more and do it better. The results? A powerful cycle of energy, achievement, more energy, and more achievement—all of which creates the image of a competent, confident individual, capable of change and growth on the job and off.

NONVERBAL IMAGE MAKERS AND BREAKERS

Carolyn wasn't faring well. Slim and well-groomed, she was complaining that her boss treated her like a little girl.

"I feel I have problems being firm," she told the other women in the seminar. "I allow myself to be manipulated, and I don't know what to do about it. I'm thirty years old. I've been married and divorced. I'm raising two small kids on my own. I'm *not* a little girl!"

One of the seminar participants said that, yes, she knew Carolyn was an adult. But strangely enough she, too, had the impression that Carolyn was very young. The other participants chimed their agreement.

Then Grace pinpointed the problem. "Carolyn," she said, "do you know you have a habit of dropping your chin when you speak? That gives you a shy look. You *do* look like an embarrassed little girl."

"That's right," someone else agreed. "And when you drop your chin, you don't look at people directly."

In the remaining weeks of the seminar, Carolyn worked on correcting her image problem. Simply by lifting her chin and maintaining eye-contact with the person she was speaking to, she transformed her image from that of a shy little girl to one of a competent adult who could take care of herself. Of course, there were also other communication skills that she had to work on. But the lowered chin and averted eyes were instrumental in creating a counterproductive image.

Carolyn started getting new responses from people. Even before the eight-week seminar was over, her boss had commented on Carolyn's changed appearance. He actually said that she seemed to have grown up! More important, he set a time for them to discuss extending Carolyn's responsibilities on the job.

Your physical image communicates messages. The images can be positive or negative. What visual messages do you communicate? How do you come across to others? The best ways to evaluate and remake your image is by taking one step at a time. The following procedure is both reasonable and effective.

• Study yourself in a mirror. How do you look standing? Sitting? Talking? Do you look confident? Scared? Professional? A mirror provides instant replay. Allow yourself to see what's good about your image, as well as what's bad. By seeing what's right, you'll be motivated to work on what's wrong. You probably spent hours studying yourself in the mirror when you were a teenager. It's time to do it again and to learn from it.

• Ask people to comment on your physical image. Other people are often the best mirrors; they allow you to see yourself clearly. In fact, you may want to form a network of friends and colleagues who provide each other with image feedback. But beware! Your aim is to gain insight from other people, not automatically accept their opinions over yours. You want to use other people's views to develop your own judgment.

• Don't try to change everything at once. You may, in fact probably will, discover more than one image problem. The mirror can be heartless! So, establish a list of priorities for the problems you want to work on. Identify the most serious and begin work on those first—one or two at a time.

• Be aware of other people's responses to your image changes: Are the changes producing the results you want? Are other people treating you differently? You may want to make further changes if you're not getting the response you want.

• Enjoy the rewards of your changed image. Try to give yourself positive reinforcement for success. Perhaps treat yourself to something special. At the very least, congratulate yourself.

The Immediate Indicators

It is estimated that at least 80 percent of any message is communicated nonverbally. Many factors contribute to how you put the message across. We feel the six major ones are carriage, handshake, eye-contact, voice, dress, and gesture. These are instant communicators which tell just where you're at.

Carriage.   Stand tall! Stomach in! Chin up! Shoulders straight! No, you're not in the army now: you're working on good posture. Posture communicates presence. *Hear I am*, it says. *All of me. Take notice: I am worth it*!

Use the mirror to take inventory on how you stand. Are your shoulders upright? Forget about shoulders back; you don't want to look like a marine sergeant. But you do want to look self-confident and worthy of respect.

Is your head held high? Not too high, but held so you look directly into someone else's eyes. If you hold it too high, you'll look uninvolved. If your head is lowered with chin nestling in your collarbone, you'll look timid and shy.

Is your stomach tucked in? You can't slouch if your stomach is in place, which is *in*. For the best posture, pull in your stomach and lift your rib cage. That forces you to lift your whole body. If you have trouble with posture, we recommend taking an exercise or ballet class. This will heighten the awareness of your body and help you to control it.

Handshake.   The handshake is a human telegraph system. It communicates your presence. It reaches out to the other person. It establishes contact on the basis of equality. Although only a gesture, it will boost your image as a serious professional and help you in your campaign to be taken seriously.

But, you may be wondering, is it right for me, a secretary, to shake hands? Is it my place to shake hands? Won't the other person think I'm ridiculous? And besides, women don't shake hands, do they?

The answers to these questions are easy. Yes, it is right to shake hands in most instances. Yes, it is your place to do so. Some people may think you're ridiculous, but many others will be impressed. And, yes, women do shake hands; especially professionals.

You're not *just* a secretary. You are a serious professional, effective in your secretarial functions and entitled to respect for your contributions to the organization. You have every right to shake hands.

The question is: In what circumstances do you shake hands and with whom?

You will have to make that determination on your own. Certainly, you will not shake hands every day as you greet your boss. But why not shake his hand when you first meet in the job interview? Wouldn't this be one way to communicate the message that you are a serious professional and expect to be treated that way?

What about your boss's visitors? How would they take to your extended hand? If you are to deal with them on a serious, professional basis, we believe a handshake is appropriate and extremely useful. It will boost your image of yourself, and it will boost your image in the eyes of most of your boss's associates. They might be surprised at first, but the majority will respond positively.

If you are hesitant about shaking hands, ask yourself what's the worst that can happen. Will the person fail or refuse to take the extended hand? Ignore you? Laugh? You can live with the embarrassment.

Extend your hand first. If you wait for the other person to initiate the handshake, you may have a very long wait. Take a risk! At least try it. You'll probably like it.

Once you decide to shake hands, do it right. Here are a few pointers:

• Grasp the other person's hand. Don't just place your hand there, use your grip.
• Bend your arm at the elbow. This allows for a friendly, assertive handshake, bringing the two of you closer. Extending the arm straight-out is a stiff, unnatural movement: it puts distance between you and the other person, instead of bridging it.

- Establish eye-contact. If you look embarrassed, the hand-shake will be embarrassing. If you act as though it's perfectly natural, chances are that the other person will agree.

It is worth your while to work on an effective, assertive hand-shake. Of course this means getting feedback from others. Practice with friends. You may be embarrassed at first but just remember you are developing an important tool for self-assertion.

Eye-Contact. Eye-contact is a powerful tool in your campaign to be taken seriously. It acts as an effective reinforcement for any act of self-assertion. A handshake without direct eye-contact is like an apple pie without apples. It's no pie—or no handshake—at all!

Comfortable eye-contact, however, covers a larger facial area than you may suspect. Think of this target area as an inverted triangle: the forehead, eyes, nose, mouth. Keep your gaze within this area, but be sure to vary your point of focus.

Eye-contact should be steady and friendly; it communicates a message of reliable, businesslike professionalism; it invites cooperative working relationships. Failure to look directly at people when speaking indicates anxiety and lack of confidence. People will be less apt to listen. Locking gazes, however, communicates a threatening message. Even your boss could be intimidated. *Dare me*! is not an attitude that encourages a cooperative working relationship.

Practice comfortable, steady eye-contact. Use your mirror at first, then practice it with a partner. If you don't know how uncomfortable a locked gaze is, try it with your partner. Lock directly on the eyes for a few moments: neither of you will like it.

Also, practice your eye-contact exercises at varying distances from your partner. Get a sense of how distance affects the power of eye-contact, and how it can be adjusted to remain an effective tool.

After your exercises with a partner, practice eye-contact within the inverted triangle with others—a friend, your boss, someone who has intimidated you. It will become an easy and natural technique in your campaign to strengthen your image. Soon it won't be a technique at all; it will be you!

Voice. Your voice speaks volumes about you; volumes that are quickly read by others. You need to know what your voice—the way you hold your mouth and form your words, the volume at which you speak— says about you if you want to shape the image you present.

Even for work on your voice, a mirror is your best friend. A tape recorder can be intimidating. A mirror, however, gives a picture of your whole self as you speak.

Are you moving your mouth? You should be. A tight mouth indicates nervousness and stiffness. A racing mouth—one that speeds through the sounds—will likewise set people on edge. A lazy mouth—one that barely bothers to form distinct sounds—will produce annoying mumbles. A relaxed, moderate motion will help you enunciate clearly and enable you to hold the attention of any size audience.

The first few words give the immediate impression. Practice several openings you can use when being introduced to someone. For example, "Hello. It's nice to meet you." Nothing fancy; just natural. Feel comfortable with the image in the mirror. Be sure not to let your greeting trail off into an embarrassed mumble before you reach the end of the sentence. This can show a real don't-bother-with-me image, making everything after it meaningless.

Once you feel comfortable with your image, you may want to use a tape recorder to get a reading on the actual sound. Better yet, use your network of colleagues. Other people are the best judges on such matters as voice volume, rate of speech, and fluency.

The volume of your voice may send a wrong message. For example, a loud voice suggests aggression, although you may not be an aggressive person; it's a turnoff. Just as much a turnoff, and possibly just as deceptive, is an overly soft voice which suggests you are intimidated, nervous, and uncertain, none of which may be true.

The correct volume of your voice depends on the closeness of the other person, the size of the room, and extraneous noise in the area. Work on developing a sense of what's appropriate. It's up to you to determine what the situation is and to adjust your voice accordingly.

Dress. What you wear can sometimes have more of an impact than all other aspects of your image put together. This is especially true if you are inappropriately dressed. You can, however, be "correctly" dressed for work by following three rules.

Dress for the environment. Snappy, trendy clothing is appropriate for, say, an advertising agency; it is out of place in a bank. Jodie learned this lesson when she worked as director of executive training for a large New York department store. One day her boss advised her to wear more stylish clothes and a greater variety of outfits. "This is a retail establishment," he reminded her, "and the employees should be models of the stylish clothing we sell."

"If you give me a raise, I'll be able to afford more clothes," Jodie replied jokingly, resenting the implicit slur on her old standbys. When she thought of this exchange in later years, she realized she had missed the point. Her clothing had reduced her effectiveness on the job: the merchandise managers and buyers she dealt with respected a fashionable image. Jodie's boss had given her good advice, but she had reacted defensively.

Some businesses require particular clothing styles. Dress in the banking or insurance industries tends to be conservative, while in the advertising or cosmetics industry it is likely to be trendy and stylish. A little on-the-spot research using simple observation will clue you in to the appropriate clothing style in an organization.

Dress for the position you aspire to. A manager in an insurance company does not wear jeans; if you insist on your right to wear jeans, you will not be considered for the position.

What job are you aiming for? Observe the clothes of the people now at that level. Are you willing to go along with that style? If that's not your style, you must rethink priorities and either readjust your attitude toward dress or aim for another type of job.

If the job takes priority, then role models will provide the clues for your appropriate dress. It's not necessary to make yourself into a carbon copy of another person, but it is necessary to study the overall impression projected by the clothing; and then wear clothes that create a similar impression.

Magazines are another good source of dress information. The ads can be as instructive as the articles. *Ms.*, *Working Women*, *Savvy*, and *Self* all focus on women with professional careers. Then, of course, there are the business and news magazines aimed at both men and women. *Fortune*, *Newsweek*, *Time*, and *Business Week*, for example, present role models of high-powered individuals.

We must add a warning, however; the image of little-girl or sexy women in lower-level positions dies slowly. A magazine catering to both men and women may perpetuate the stale image of the male boss dressed to project authority and a female secretary dressed to project cuteness or sexiness. Stay away from a blatantly sexy image. Long, garish fingernails, heavy perfume, and heavy eye shadow are no-no's in almost any industry, including cosmetics. And avoid tottering along the corridor in four-inch heels. Can you take a person seriously when she totters? She looks vulnerable, and remember: a vulnerable image works against upward mobility.

And finally, those of you aspiring to move up the career ladder may be wondering about designer labels. Will they help you to be taken seriously? After all, the high price tag must mean that you think enough of yourself to spend a fortune on your clothes. Right? Not exactly. It's not the labels that count; it's the appropriate style. You don't need a label for a style that projects an image of quality and authority.

Dress appropriately every day. Dressing for the formal job interview is important. It communicates a message about how you see yourself, and where. But good grooming and appropriate dress extends beyond the interview. It means dressing appropriately every single day. The next time you want to wear your jeans and a sport shirt on the job, think about the message you are sending to a boss looking to fill an assistant buyer's slot.

Perhaps you feel offended by dress codes, formal or informal. Before you start waving the banner of dress liberation, though, consider the price and decide whether you want to pay it. What if your clothes hurt your chances to get a much-desired job? What if your dress raises a barrier to career advancement? The key is to place yourself in an environment where you feel comfortable. Then adhering to the dress code of the organization will not be an unbearable restraint but a natural situation.

Gestures. We have already discussed the importance of a handshake. That gesture enhances the image of a career professional. So does the occasional use of your hands to emphasize a point during formal speeches or even in everyday conversation.

Many gestures, however, are merely distracting mannerisms. For example, do you play with your hair? Twirl it? Fix it? Fluff it? Push it out of your eyes? Play with barrettes? Do you play with rings, bracelets, or other jewelry? Twirl them? Pull them off and on? Do you touch your face? Scratch your head? Fidget? Shuffle from one foot to the other? Jingle change in your pockets? Bite your nails? Bite your lips? Make wild hand gestures?

Hand gestures should be used to make a point. If yours don't, give them up.

Nonverbal indicators of image—carriage, handshake, eye-contact, voice, dress, and gestures—have an impact on how you are preceived. In the next chapter, we explore the verbal factor of effective communication. When used together, verbal and nonverbal communication show that you are ready, willing, and able to move ahead in your career.

Chapter Four

Communicating Effectively

Compare these three statements:

"I'm kind of unhappy about my salary, and I feel I should have a raise."

"I've just been working so hard—being your secretary and now also doing the filing and typing and phone answering and, you know, all the secretarial work for George since his secretary was laid off, and all. You know, I really think I deserve a raise. I really feel that strongly."

"I've been doing George's secretarial work in addition to yours for six months. I've taken on more responsibilities and I've fulfilled them. I feel I deserve a raise."

All three statements get across the idea that the secretary wants a raise. But only the third will make a boss sit up and take notice that the secretary deserves to be taken seriously as a career professional.

That is not to say that the other two might not result in more money. A boss hearing the first message might give a raise because she feels sorry for the secretary. In the second situation, pity and egotism might lead her to decide that such loyal hard work and dedication deserve some financial recognition.

In the third situation, however, the secretary has made a statement—clear, concise, straightforward, rational, and persuasive. There were no fancy words, no complicated ideas. It communicates the message in a professional, businesslike manner. Your boss can understand that message. And respect it! (For more on salary negotiation, see p. 162.)

Effective verbal communication is a very important factor in projecting a successful image. It has two major elements: what you say and how you listen.

THE CORE STATEMENT

When does a sentence, or string of sentences, become a statement? Statements are taken seriously, and people who make them are likewise taken seriously.

Do secretaries make statements? Not often enough. But they can and should! A statement should be used in a variety of situations—for example, when informing other people of your skills, interests, career goals, and career action plans; when making a request for a raise, a career research interview, additional training; and when issuing instructions.

We're talking here about a core statement: a single controlling thought on which other remarks are built. The message should come through strong and clear. In effect, the statement acts like an anchor, giving you stability, holding you firmly to your position.

The statement helps you avoid the manipulative traps that are all too prevalent in office games. With a statement, you define your point of view. You can listen to and empathize with the other person's ideas while still focusing on your needs and interests. The other person will be compelled to deal with you as an independent individual whose point of view must be respected and, if not accepted, at least dealt with on its merits. You cannot be simply dismissed!

The statement is a powerful tool in projecting the image of a serious career professional capable of making tough decisions, solving tough problems, and assuming greater responsibility and authority.

Statement Weakeners

Many words and phrases dilute your serious image and lessen the immediacy of your message. Secretaries often use these. They are the tentative phrases and words, the modifiers, the artificial props which many people believe offer a more gracious, less pushy way to express a need, an idea, or a feeling. Secretaries who believe this are not only diluting their message, they're deluding themselves. Nine times out of ten the only result of using those modifiers will be dismissal of your ideas—and your seriousness.

Use of ''diluters'' is a habit you can change. To begin with, stop using *but*. *But* is one of the most common qualifiers. Using it sometimes to express contrast, objection, or conflict is appropriate; however, it often paralyzes and raises problems which don't exist.

Consider the counterproductive use of "but" in the following examples:

> Yes, but . . .
> No, but . . .
> But I don't know what . . .
> But you don't understand . . .
> I have had lots of experience, but . . .
> I want to be in sales, but . . .
> I love working with people, but . . .

Other qualifiers are:

> kind of—"I *kind of* want to do more work with people."
> sort of—"I'd *sort of* like to go."
> really—"I *really* want to work more with people."
> just—"I *just* feel that I want to work more with
>   people."
> I think/I don't think—"*I don't think* I want to work more with people."
> I'm not sure—"I'm *not sure* I want to."
> I guess—"*I guess* I could."

These tentatives are poison. Stay away from them completely.

Apologies, Apologies

Confident professionalism on the job is never having to say you're sorry. Self-effacement does not work for the serious professional on the way up. People who apologize too often are not taken seriously.

The secretary has a long tradition of preceived weakness on the job: she can't be trusted to make independent judgments, she must have orders to follow and so on. Apologies reinforce this perception of the secretary as weak.

Apologizing can be almost a reflex. People who lack confidence will apologize rather than assert, explain, request, argue, or act. The apologizer relies on apology instead of effective communication. Sample apologies include:

> I hate to ask you, but . . .

I'm sorry to bring this up, but . . .
I hope I'm not bothering you, but . . .
I know you're busy, but . . .
I'm sorry to take your time, but . . .
You may think I'm being overly sensitive, but . . .

Notice that these apologetic phrases are coupled with the word *but*, a sure sign of weak communication. *Just*, *but*, and *sorry* are strong clues that you are not using core statements.

How to Phrase a Core Statement

When you strip your sentences of useless qualifiers, tentatives, apologies, self-doubts, and fears, what are you left with? A straightforward statement. Don't worry! You won't be speechless; you'll be saying what you think. Compare these two examples:

> "I'm sorry to disturb you, but I would really appreciate the chance to discuss with you the possibility of utilizing some suggestions for making better use of my time. I kind of picked up a number of pointers in my time-management seminar. Could you possibly spare some time for me at two this afternoon? It's kind of really important to me."
>
> "I want to talk to you about some suggestions I have for making better use of my time. I picked up a number of pointers in my time-management seminar. How about getting together at two this afternoon? It's important to me."

Take the plunge into statements. Think out what you want to say. Use your own words. Don't use long sentences or difficult words—you want people to understand you: long-winded sentences will lose them. So will those "impressive" words that most people have never heard, let alone used.

Make the statement specific. Use concrete words, concrete facts, concrete suggestions.

Notice that the statement began with:

• What the secretary wanted: "to talk to you"
• The purpose: to discuss suggestions "for making better use of my time." (It's best if the purpose indicates some benefit for the other person.)

Then came the background information:

• She picked up the suggestions "in my time-management seminar." (This background also tells the listener that participation in the seminar paid off—particularly relevant if the organization paid for the secretary to attend.)

Finally came specific proposals and reason(s) behind them:

• "getting together at two this afternoon"
• "It's important to me."

Exercises. Perform a similar analysis of the statements at the beginning of this chapter, in which the secretary asks for a raise. Pay attention to what information was conveyed in each part of the statement and why this needed to be conveyed.

Practice writing your own core statements. First think them through. Then write down the essential points. Practice saying them aloud to yourself. Do they sound natural? Persuasive? Look at yourself in the mirror. Do you look natural? Confident? Check your posture, eye-contact, lip movements, and watch for distracting gestures.

Next, practice the statements with other people in your network. Do they see and hear the statements as you do? Do they see and hear them as you intended? Analyze what's right with the statements and what's wrong with them, too.

Finally, use the statements with other people—your boss, an associate, a subordinate. The more you use them, the easier and more effective they will become. Integrate them as a regular communication tool throughout your professional career.

As you use statements more often and more effectively, you will find that others will understand you better, listen to you more attentively, and take you more seriously. You will also find others responding more clearly and more directly. In short, your statements can foster a chain of effective communication. Everyone benefits!

EFFECTIVE LISTENING

"I learned to listen as a secretary because often I had to follow very specific directions." Nancy identified listening as the most important skill that she transferred from her secretarial experience to her position as top salesperson for a New Jersey radio station. "If I didn't understand the directions, or if they were incomplete," she continued, "I learned to clarify them. That was very important training for sales."

"*Now,*" she says, "I listen to potential customers. I have to know what they want so they'll buy radio time from me." Today Nancy gets daily confirmation of how valuable her listening skills are.

Listening is a vastly underrated communication skill. People think listening comes naturally. It doesn't! However, the skill can be acquired through training and experience.

A good listener projects the image of a thoughtful, responsible, and capable professional. People who listen carefully can absorb, digest, and evaluate more effectively. Always aware of what the other person is saying, the good listener gives appropriate feedback and gets it as well.

An effective listener uses active and passive techniques. Both let the speaker know you hear what is being said. Active listening is reflective listening—it encourages the other person to open up. Passive techniques work more as a seal of understanding; let's look at these techniques first.

Passive Techniques

Passive listening does not mean sitting back and doing nothing while the other person speaks. You can participate in the conversation without talking. How? Passive listening techniques give clues to the other person. The clues communicate understanding, lack of understanding, approval, disapproval, interest, boredom, and so on. The most common clues are:

Facial gestures—smiles, frowns, grimaces, raised eyebrows
Head movements—nods of assent and dissent
Sounds—Uh huh, hmmm, sighs, groans
Body gestures—shrugging, relaxing, tensing up
Hand gestures—raising or pointing a finger, clenching a fist

Use these clues to communicate with the other person. But also "listen" to these clues from the other person. They will guide you to the real message.

Active Techniques

Active listening techniques allow you to comment and seek clarification about what the other person has said. The two major techniques are the clarifying question and the clarifying statement.

On a job interview, where effective listening is essential, your prospective boss might say, "I have a lot of personal correspondence that you would be responsible for." A clarifying question you could respond with is, "What do you mean by 'personal correspondence'?"

Perhaps you think you know what your prospective boss means by personal correspondence. Thinking you know is not enough. You must know *exactly*—or assume responsibility for your failure to find out.

Another example:

BOSS: This job is very demanding.
YOU: Could you give me some examples of what you mean?
BOSS: You will sometimes have to work weekends.
YOU: Should I expect that to happen often?
BOSS: No.

Your first question—asking for examples of what was meant—required the prospective boss to be specific. You found out one example of what he was talking about. Did your second question give you the information you needed? No! To this boss, "often" may mean once or twice a month, whereas to you it may mean once in two or three months.

Avoid this trap by asking more specific questions. In this example, you might ask, "How often should I expect that to happen?" The boss should give a specific answer—and then you can determine if his idea of "often" corresponds to yours.

But if you get an ambiguous answer, all is not lost. If you listen and realize you didn't get a specific answer, follow up with another clarifying question. Suppose he responded, "Not often." Then you can pin him down by mentioning a specific figure. "Five or six times a year?" you might ask. Or, you might use both a clarifying statement and a clarifying question: "It's important that I understand what you mean by 'not often.' Could I expect that to happen, say, five or six times a year?"

Or you can define your needs—offering free information about yourself: "I would not want to work on weekends more than five or six times a year. Is that what you mean by 'not often'?"

In that situation, you have disclosed your own interpretation of "often" and "not often." If he disagrees, you may have lost the job. On the other hand, if you did not want to work on weekends more than five or six times a year, you didn't want to be his secretary anyway. In any event, you will understand what is expected of you and he will understand what you are willing to do.

Active listening involves not just hering words, but understanding what they mean—to you and to the other person. In the job interview, you understood the words "no" and "not often." You did not, however, understand what they meant in concrete terms.

Free Information.   In the above example, you offered free information—free gifts of self-disclosure about your needs. You gave a more subtle bit of free information when you said it was "important" that you understand what the prospective boss meant by "not often." You were disclosing one of your values without having been asked. You told him a little about yourself.

In good conversation *both* parties offer free information. Picking up on free information requires that you be alert; read between the lines; hear not only the words but the meaning behind them—and sometimes, the *real* meaning behind that. If your boss gives you a report to type, she might simply ask you to type it. Or, she might say that this is a very important report. The "very important" is free information, alerting you that she probably wants an extra special typing job. Or, she might say that this report "will determine the whole future of the company." The message: the report must be perfect—no mistakes will be tolerated.

If you are not sure what the free information means, find out. It's your boss's responsibility to communicate clearly, but it's your responsibility to make sure you understand what she wants.

Don't be afraid the other person will think you are stupid if you ask questions. The clarifying questions and statements show your concern, and your image will be stronger as a result.

More Pointers on Effective Listening

1. Let a person finish a statement or question before you comment. Sometimes the most important part comes at the end. If you interrupt, you might get only half the message—and miss the *real* meaning.
2. Slow down your responses to the other person's questions. Think about your answer. If you don't have an answer immediately, there's nothing wrong with saying you need to think about the question a little, or you don't know the answer now but will find out. Active listening does not mean quick responses but *appropriate* responses. Rushing in with an answer when you're uncertain is a defensive reaction; admitting you don't know can show self-confidence and good sense.
3. Stop worrying about what you'll say. If you listen well, pick up on free information, and then think about your response, you will find that good communication follows. You will understand

the other person; the other person will understand you. *That* is effective communication.

4. Don't be afraid of silence. Silence often means assent or at least consideration of your point of view. Even after getting a positive response, some people keep on making the same point over and over. That's boring, and it shows lack of confidence all too clearly. Some of communication is knowing when to stop talking.

A successful image requires effective communication. And effective communication is essential for anyone who wants to be taken seriously.

Communication patterns are habits: if faulty, they can be changed; if good, they should be reinforced. It is important to become aware of your habits and work on making them effective.

Chapter Five

Office Games— and How to Overcome Them

RESPONSIBILITY WITHOUT AUTHORITY

Now that you have begun to work on your image and communication skills, you need to turn your attention to the forces operating around you—your boss, your boss's boss, your co-workers. Even after you've inventoried your skills and examined your image, things still may not go right. You may find yourself caught up in office games, and only professional savvy and strong interpersonal skills will allow you to break the traditional patterns which "keep you in your place."

You are secretary to the vice president in charge of personnel. It's your responsibility to arrange for part-time and temporary help. You work within a strict budget. In theory, your boss authorizes all arrangements involving expenditure of extra funds. In reality, however, you have taken on much of this responsibility.

One week a marketing VP tells your boss that he absolutely, positively needs a full-time temp to help his secretary catch up on a backlog of paperwork. Your boss is, as usual, very busy. He tells you to "handle it."

You see the problems immediately. Hiring a temp for a thirty-five-hour week will put you over budget. But didn't your boss tell you to handle it? Doesn't that mean the marketing VP must get his temp? Aren't those, in effect, your boss's orders? And don't you have to follow your boss's orders?

Unsure about what to do, you finally hire a temp for a thirty-five-hour week. The next Friday, you get a call from the controller. "Who gave *you* authority to go over budget?" he yells.

"Why didn't you check with me first?" your boss asks.

What's happening in this situation? How can you, as secretary, improve your position?

Several important forces are at work. Let's look at each of these briefly, then we'll examine losing and winning moves.

Responsibility Without Authority.   We mean *your* responsibility and *your* authority. Clearly your boss has confidence in you, otherwise he would not have handed over his responsibility for making decisions. But he has handed over responsibility and not the formal authority to act. In effect, you are simply "helping him out." Without the authority you are caught in a very tricky situation. If things go right, you don't get the credit: if things go wrong, you do get the blame. It's a guaranteed no-win dilemma.

Your Boss's Authority.   What *is* your boss's authority? Might he, too, be stymied by responsibility without authority? Does he have to clear all expenditures through the controller, or does he have independent authority for expenditures? How does his status within the organization affect you? Is he likely to support you in a conflict between you and another individual or department?

Unclear Orders.   Unclear orders are dangerous to your health. As we discussed in the preceeding chapter, a good listener will ask a clarifying question when faced with unclear orders (if you skipped the last chapter, go back to it). You shouldn't have to deal with unclear orders; they are extremely stressful and dangerous to your health!

Independent Judgment.   You have the capacity for judgment, judgment that may differ from your boss's. You have the right to independent judgment.

You not only have the right, but the obligation—to yourself, your boss, and your organizaton—to evaluate a situation in light of the information available to you. For example, you knew that hiring a full-time temp would put you over budget. Perhaps your boss—conveniently or not—forgot that fact. You also knew the marketing VP needed a full-time temp. The controller did not know that. You were a clearinghouse for all the facts of the situation.

WINNING STRATEGIES

How would *you* handle the authority conflict involving the temp? When your boss tells you to "handle it," what would you do?

Let's look first at some of the losing moves in an authority conflict.

You might:

- Let it slide—say and do nothing, knowing that the marketing

VP and his secretary will somehow resolve the problem (probably through extra hours put in by the secretary).
• Say you'll take care of it, but do nothing.
• Say you'll take care of it and hire the extra temp without reminding your boss of the budgetary constraints.
• Say, "I can't do it" and give no explanation.
• Cry—from fear and frustration.
• Scream and insult your boss for not knowing his job or the bind he has put you in.
• Hire the temp, but badmouth your boss for being weak, stupid, and for not standing up for you.
• Retaliate: don't go to work the next day.
• Hire the temp—and feel pleased that you saved your boss from a potential embarrassment.
• Find out what is usually done in such a situation and do it without looking for a better way.

Each of these moves—and there are undoubtedly more—represents a failure in communication and a losing style of behavior. Each of them reveals unwillingness to face the conflict in the situation—and risk a creative confrontation in order to find the best solution. What is behind this avoidance of confrontation? Fear of anger, desire for approval, a need to always be perfect, and reluctance to take risks.

But look again. Few people enjoy experiencing someone else's anger, most seek the approval of others, few *want* to make mistakes, and the majority of people want to be safe. So, there is nothing particularly troublesome about this, right? Wrong!

The question is one of degree. Secretaries in a rut have an extreme fear of anger, an extreme desire for approval, an extreme need to be thought perfect, an extreme reluctance to take risks. Secretaries, like everyone else, need to develop the ability to weigh the facts in a given situation and take reasonable action based on evaluation of those facts.

How do you determine if there *is* a genuine conflict? Unfortunately, there are no magic formulas. Identifying the facts and weighing them before taking action are at the core of a winning strategy for conflict situations. Your first task is to recognize that you are in such a situation.

When you find yourself facing a problem that's your business to solve, and which won't simply go away, there are reasonable procedures you can follow to solve it. Let's see how they work when we apply them.

Identify the Facts.   Your best bet is to lay out all the facts. Here, they would look like this:

1. The VP wants a full-time temp to help out on a heavy work load.
2. The boss tells you to handle it.
3. Your budget does not allow for a full-time temp.
4. You lack the authority to go over budget without your boss's OK.
5. The controller is a stickler for keeping within budget.

Weigh the Facts.   Look clearly at the facts in this situation. Are some more important than others? Are you overlooking a significant detail, for example, a power struggle between the controller and your boss? Is your boss's job secure or has there been evidence that he's on the way down or out?

State the Problem.   You can't reach a conclusion until you can state the problem. State it as simply as possible. In this case, if you've identified a power struggle involving your boss, you could say, "I'm caught in a conflict of authority between my boss and the controller. My problem is, I don't have the authority to 'handle it' on my own."

Identify and Evaluate Alternatives for Action.   Once you've determined you lack the authority to handle the problem, you must lay out your options. We suggest two:

1. Go to your boss, explain the conflict (VP's needs vs. budgetary constraints), and recommend a course of action.
2. Get out of the problem—say no to your boss or to the VP. State your reasons.

Weigh the pros and cons of each of your options.

If you take option one—spell out facts, recommend a solution, and let your boss make the decision—you have worked within the current limits of your authority without posing a threat. By suggesting a solution, you have demonstrated your problem-solving ability and, if it's adopted, you can set a precedent for your expanded role in similar situations. If it happens repeatedly you'll eventually want to rewrite your job description to formally clarify and extend your authority.

If you take option two—say no to the VP or to your boss—you end your participation in the problem and will waste no more time or energy on it. Stating your reasons will give the facts to the other principals.

Choose the Best Alternative. Weigh the possible conflicts of needs and claims—yours, your boss's, your organization's. Now, decide which alternative is best.

Follow Through. Once you determine your best alternative, you must follow through with action. One form of follow-through is to ''stage'' a creative confrontation that will lead to resolution of the problem (more on creative confrontations in chapter 7).

By making the problems and issues clear, you make it possible for everyone to concentrate on real organizational interests and stop seeing the situation as one in which one person wins and everyone else loses. You rewrite the rules and cancel the game.

Authority conflicts are among the most common—and serious—of all office games. Secretaries often get caught in these conflicts. Do you recognize the situation? Do you play by ''the rules''? Or do you rewrite them—in your favor?

There are two fundamental rules affecting secretaries in this game; both work against your best interests. In fact, these rules are against the best interests of your boss and your organization—but too often they don't realize it.

RULE 1: *Subordinate your needs to your boss's.* In effect, this rule says that your boss is numero uno. Your boss's needs are top priority, and whatever the boss does is in the organization's best interest. The underlying assumption is that *you* cannot possibly know the organization's best interests.

RULE 2: *Don't think. Just do as you are told!* If the boss's needs are in tune with the organization's best interests, it follows logically that the boss's judgment can be trusted and yours can't. If your judgment can't be trusted, then your role is simply to follow orders. And don't bother pointing out conflicts between those orders and office realities. You don't really understand what your boss is after!

REWRITE THE RULES

So, you are handed iron-tight, infallible rules. It seems as though you have no choice but to follow them. But you do have choices! Since you can learn to recognize the game, and modify your image, you can rewrite the rules.

Seek Choices. There is no *one* right way to handle any situation.

You are in a position to help your boss. As secretary, you are often more aware of office problems than your boss is. You are also closer to the people—the other secretaries and clerical help—who must cope with them. You can therefore suggest reasonable alternatives when you see problems.

You can—and should—use your judgment to evaluate a situation, evaluate your boss's decision, and offer feedback on both the situation and the decision. You are an office expert! Expert opinions are much valued. Value yours, and chances are that your boss will, too. If your boss doesn't, weigh that factor in your evaluation of your boss: it may be time for you to move on to a boss who will allow you to use all of your abilities.

Understand Consequences. Your action and inaction have consequences. If your boss says, "Do it!" and you do, realize that there are consequences both for doing it and not doing it. What are these consequences?

Obviously they will depend on the situation. In this chapter, your boss told you to "handle it." You did, although you understood right away that there were big problems. You satisfied the marketing VP, but you went over budget, you angered the controller, your boss disavowed your action, and you were left isolated. You won few points for following your boss's "order," even though you played by the rules.

And what if you hadn't followed orders? The controller probably would not have been brought into this particular office drama—at least not until the marketing VP's backlog started having bottom-line consequences. Probably the VP would have been angry. The important consequence for you, however, would have been how it affected your relationship with your boss. Perhaps your boss would have been angry, even distrustful of you. If you did not communicate your reasons for not following orders, your boss might have suspected sabotage (even though in this situation following orders would have been the clearer case of sabotage).

Identify Needs. Everybody has needs—this is true of your boss, your coworkers, your subordinates, you. Your boss's needs do not necessarily take precedence over yours; your boss's best interests are not necessarily those of the organization. They may be, but yours may be, too.

What are examples of your needs? The most important are:

- gaining the respect of others
- keeping—or gaining—self-respect

- having challenging responsibilities and the authority to meet them
- having a salary appropriate to your responsibilities
- learning and growing on the job.

Redefine Winning. Winning is working with others to get the best possible solution for the organization, for your boss, and for yourself.

Forget about the fear that if you win, your boss loses—and that no boss will tolerate that and let you keep your job. If you have this win/lose mentality, you will probably be too afraid to speak up for yourself and your needs. Then you will be the loser.

Cultivate a Winning Style. The winning style relies on straightforward communication—treating others with respect and insisting they treat you likewise. The secretary with a winning style knows she has brains, and she is not afraid to use them. She exercises independent judgment.

You can cultivate a winning style. But it requires courage and willingness to take risks. It is much easier to continue old patterns—even if they are holding you back—than to exchange them for new ones which will help you get ahead. But playing office games by the old rules and with a self-limiting style is not playing smart. The smart strategy is to rewrite the rules and cultivate a winning style that allows you to share in a joint victory.

Chapter Six

More Games—and Winning Strategies to Deal with Them

MANIPULATIVE CRITICISM

Now that the classic responsibility-without-authority game has been won, it's time to examine other office situations that can deflate your self-image. Manipulative criticism, overprotection, failure to give recognition, and your own reluctance to take charge can keep you chained to no-growth jobs. Changing the rules of these games is your only way out.

You are secretary to a senior account executive at a leading ad agency. Your boss is brilliant and demanding. "I've made it to the top because I demand perfection," she said when she hired you.

"Well, she warned me!" you moan on a particularly difficult day. "But I had no idea it would be this tough. I can't seem to do anything right!" That morning she returned two letters that you had drafted for her to sign: "These are terrible!" she said. "My clients will think I'm a dumb cluck." Then she rushed off to a client meeting. In parting, she called back, "And when are you going to learn how to make a decent cup of coffee?"

You examine the letters. In one, you had misused a word, using "effect" instead of "affect." In the other you could find nothing wrong. "Why does she think they're terrible?" you ask yourself. "One misused word is not a catastrophe. And she really meant to imply that *I* am a dumb cluck, didn't she? If only I could please her. If only I could think like her . . ."

What's happening in this situation? You have been criticized, you don't really understand the criticism, you are ready to accept your boss's implied judgment that you can't do anything right, and you are suffering. There are three forces at work here: manipulation, masochism, and self-respect.

Manipulation. Criticism can hurt or it can help. You must weed out the criticism that only hurts and encourage you boss to give you helpful criticism. You can learn from positive, constructive criticism; you can grow from it. And it aids you in building a dynamic career.

Negative criticism, on the other hand, tears you down and intimidates you. It can stand in the way of your self-development—both on the job and off. Negative criticism is a great manipulator; it ties you in knots because it gets you to do or believe something without realizing what's going on. The secretary in the ad agency, for example, was manipulated into a state of extreme anxiety and insecurity. Numbed by a stream of criticism, she lost her sense of competence and self-worth and her ability to see that her boss was, clearly, running her in circles.

Dealing with criticism is a serious problem. It's important to learn to use criticism as a learning device. It is also important to avoid being manipulated by criticism. You must exercise your judgment. If the criticism is way off base, see it as such and point out the shortcomings to the person dishing it out. If the criticism is valid, learn from it and make the appropriate changes.

Masochism. Many people with fine skills crumble under criticism even when it's thoroughly unfair. They display masochism. In other words, they passively accept being stepped on.

Secretaries often get so used to abuse they start to think of it as normal. At the same time, however, they complain that they are not appreciated, that their work is undervalued, that they don't get respect. It's time for secretaries to get their act together—either stop acting like a wet rag or stop complaining about being dumped on. We're in favor of shucking the masochism.

Self-Respect. The key to protection from negative criticism and masochistic tendencies lies in self-respect and feeling pride in your work. And the key to pride lies in doing a good job and knowing that it's a good job. That takes independent judgment. It's not just up to your boss to evaluate your work, it's up to you, too. And it's up to you to evaluate your boss's criticism of your work. You have a right to evalute your work. In fact, you have a duty to evaluate it—a duty to yourself and your future.

Strategies

How would you have dealt with the overcritical boss in the advertising agency? Let's look first at some of the losing moves:

• Apologize effusively. In fact, you might apologize whenever you are criticized. The apology eventually becomes automatic.

• Cry. You have let your boss down; you are heartbroken; you cry—it becomes a chain reaction.

• Say nothing, do nothing (except sulk), and stay locked into your losing style.

• Apologize and ask coworkers how they would have done the letters—in effect, stick to the "tried and true" way of doing things.

• Counterattack. "What's wrong with the letters?" you might yell. "You gave me the information." Perhaps make excuses—"I'm too busy to see everything." Or speak scornfully—"My, we certainly are picky today."

• Quit. This is a move of desperation, although it may be easier than adopting the winning moves. As you will see, however, quitting can be a winning move, too.

OK, now let's look into the moves that will allow you to handle an overcritical boss.

Clarify the Criticism.   Don't be defensive about criticism. Find out exactly what your boss objects to. Assume you were the secretary in the situation described earlier; you discovered one error. Your task is to find out whether your boss objects to anything else in the letters.

The first step in clarifying criticism is to ask a simple question, such as, "What don't you like about the letters?" Your tone in posing this question is very important—it must not be accusatory. There's a world of difference between asking, "What don't you like about the letters?" and asking, "What's wrong with them? *You* gave me that information."

If you know you made a mistake—such as using "effect" instead of "affect"—admit it and don't dwell on it. There's nothing shameful about making errors. The old saw, "nobody's perfect," applies to you—and to your boss. What is vital in admitting a mistake, however, is the manner in which you do it. Use a strong voice and good eye-contact. If you seem scared, you will make the error appear more important than it is.

At the same time that you admit the mistake, express your willingness to correct it—immediately, if possible. Speed is important. If you can fix the error quickly, it could not have been all that terrible. If the error is more difficult to fix, express your willingness to get to work on it immediately. This reaction will show your good faith; it will usually deflect anger as well as contempt.

It's wise to avoid any kind of explanation of how and why you made the error. Even saying something like, "I guess it slipped by''—which shows that you do know what is right—nevertheless prolongs discussion of the error. Your objective is to end that discussion as quickly as possible.

And finally, in admitting a mistake, stay away from apologies, even quick and perfunctory ones like, "Sorry! I did make a mistake." Yes, you are big enough to admit when you are wrong, and we've already recommended that you admit it. "Well," you might continue, "I'm also big enough to apologize for it." But why? What does an apology do for you? No one *likes* to make mistakes. Even the simplest "sorry," can be a trap for the secretary: you put yourself in a submissive position by saying you are sorry. Instead, simply admit the error and correct it.

But to continue with our clarification of the criticism, you still don't know why your boss dismissed the letters as "terrible". You've identified just one error. Your goal, now that you've admitted the error you found, is to draw out specific, constructive criticism.

YOU: The misused word was only in one of the letters. Is there anything else wrong with either of the two letters? *(Ask questions.)*

BOSS: Yes, but I can't put my finger on it.

YOU: Are the facts wrong? *(Probe.)*

BOSS: No.

YOU: Is it the beginning? The end? The sentence structure? *(Probe deeper, be specific.)*

BOSS: Noooo . . . not exactly.

YOU: Is it too formal?

BOSS: Yes, that's it. I'm trying to develop a warm business relationship with Joe Marks and that letter makes me sound too stiff and cold.

YOU: Is there anything else you don't like about the letters? *(Don't rush away; pinpoint all the boss's objections.)*

BOSS: No, I think that's it.

YOU: Let me make sure I understand you exactly. Am I right that your objections to the letters are the misused word and the formal tone? *(Tie it up. Summarize your understanding of the boss's objections.)*

BOSS: That's it.

Evaluate the Criticism.   Decide if the criticism is fair. Evaluation goes hand in hand with the clarification of criticism. Dividing the two is somewhat artificial. For example, before you admitted the misuse of a word in the clarification stage, you had decided that you *did* err.

Thus, along with the clarification and evaluation comes the need to decide on your response. If the criticism is fair, as we have already stated, admit the mistake and correct it as quickly as possible. But what if you disagree?

Suppose, for example, that you're not convinced the tone of the letter is too formal. Suppose, in fact, you feel the tone is just right. Should you argue the point?

No! Defending yourself could lead to becoming defensive, which is a no-win tactic. Besides, this really isn't a case of right and wrong; it's a case of preferred tone. Since your boss is the one to sign the letter, she must determine whether the tone suits her.

So, what do you do? Agree with the possibility. In the earlier dialogue, you might have ended by saying, "It's possible the tone *is* too formal. I'll work on it." Alternatively, you could respond, "I can see how you might feel that way. I'll work on it."

But remember, when you agree with the possibility, adopt a style of strength and dignity. Use a calm, clear voice, maintain steady eye-contact with your boss, and make sure your facial expression is composed.

Why does this move—admitting the possibility—work in this situation? Remember, we're dealing with a very critical boss. The boss uses criticism as a manipulative tool that keeps you running in circles, ties you in knots. It keeps you in your place—which is under her thumb! Agreeing with the possibililty allows you to slip out from under her thumb. It allows you to get on with your job instead of arguing about which one of you is wrong. In most cases, people who use criticism as a manipulative tool get a kick out of the power implicit in controlling someone. In effect, you have acted to prevent your boss from playing the power game and from running you in circles.

"But," you may say, "I've lost. I've capitualted without a fight. What kind of 'strength' does that show—to give up at the start?"

The point is, you have used your judgment to determine that your boss might be right. You've also sized up the situation realistically. She is your boss; she does have authority over you; she has the right to exercise her own taste. Why fight under these circumstances? Isn't it stronger to save your fight for another type of situation, one in which you can win?

In another case, you might want to agree to the possibility that your boss is right even if you know she's wrong, in order to gain time to gather the information that proves you are right. The delay allows you to prepare for a creative confrontation during which you can defend yourself without being defensive. You will be able to present yourself as thorough and businesslike, not "emotional".

Confront Your Boss. Once you have gathered the necessary facts, present your "case". The confrontation should take place soon after the conflict surfaced. The speed with which you gather the relevant information shows that the matter is important to you.

Two other points about creative confrontation need to be mentioned here. Don't present your supporting evidence in an accusatory manner (the "See, I was right!" approach). And don't present your evidence in public. Use your strongest image, your most businesslike approach, and marshal all the pertinent facts—then make your presentation. (Creative confrontation will be covered in depth in chapter 7.)

Confront Negative Criticism. What if your boss's criticism becomes unbearable? You have admitted errors; corrected mistakes; agreed with the possibility that your boss was right; presented courteous, reasoned cases in your favor; and still the criticism continues—a steady stream of complaints, some important, many picky. Suppose you decide you can't put up with this criticism much longer.

This situation also calls for a confrontation—a free, open discussion. It is time to level with your boss. It is time to say this constant criticism is having negative effects on your self-image and your job performance. How to do it without angering or alienating your boss?

First, concentrate on the effects of the criticism. Emphasize your job performance. If you stress that the criticism not only is not spurring you to "perfection" but is actually interfering with your effectiveness on the job, your boss will stop and think about what you're saying. If you can get your boss to understand that this criticism is hindering your job performance, he or she will be more likely to see that such criticism hurts not only your effectiveness but your boss's effectiveness as well.

Second, begin your opening sentence of the confrontation with "I". Be sure to cite specific examples of how the criticism affects your behavior. Your best bet is to say something like: "I'm finding it tough to work for you because of all the criticism. Frankly, it's hard for me to concentrate on my priorities. I'm actually afraid to hand my work in. And I'm afraid to take initiative because you'll probably criticize me."

Third, give concrete examples of the type of criticism you find counterproductive. Things like put-downs (Your boss asks for a file.

You give it to him in ten minutes. He says, "Why were you so slow?"), second-guessing (Your boss constantly criticizes the way you handle details of office procedure even though, objectively, they make no difference to overall effectiveness.), and irrelevant personal criticism (comments such as "Looks like you had a late night, huh? Just don't let your extracurricular activities interfere with your job.") are the sort of snide, picayune comments that have driven many a secretary out of the office or out of her mind.

Citing these as examples of negative criticism translates into constructive criticism on your part. In effect, you are telling your boss that these comments don't help you on the job—and they don't help your boss either.

Start Thinking About Quitting.   If, despite all your efforts, the negative criticism continues, you face an important decision: whether or not you want to—and can—work for a boss who is super-critical and who constantly undermines your self-esteem.

Weigh the pros and cons of staying on the job. Questions to ask yourself include:

- What are you learning from your boss?
- What are you learning from this job: about the industry, professional behavior, etc.?
- Have you decided on your career objectives?
- Will remaining in this job improve your chances of finding a better job, with this firm or elsewhere?
- What are the chances of lining up another job soon?

Confront your boss again. This confrontation is essentially a last warning that you will quit if the criticism isn't curbed. However, you must couch your language in nonthreatening terms so that you don't maneuver your boss into a defensive position. The message to get across is that you cannot continue to work under these conditions. At the same time, begin looking for another job. Explore the market outside your organization or explore the possibility of switching to another job within.

If the criticism continues and your self-esteem is at stake, and if you cannot locate a better job within the organization, you are ready for the ultimate winning move.

Quit.   We don't advocate this move lightly. It really is a move of last resort. But you have taken various constructive steps and have determined that you cannot continue to work for this boss without completely losing your self-esteem.

If you do decide to quit, try to line up another job first. You're in a much stronger job-hunting position when you are already working. If you're without a job and your finances are shaky (which is often the case with secretaries), you are likely to grab the first job offered—and you might well end up working for a boss not much better than the one you left.

When you learn to handle criticism intelligently, you'll have learned one of life's most important survival techniques. Allowing yourself to be manipulated by criticism will interfere with your ability to do a good job. And, ultimately, it will stunt your professional growth because it will destroy your belief in yourself and your will to get ahead.

The fact remains that just because your boss is trying to manipulate you does not mean she or he will succeed. A whole series of winning moves are at your disposal. Choose the ones that are right for your situation.

AVOIDING DEPENDENCE

You are secretary to the managing editor at a publishing company. You adore your boss. You feel so protected working for him. He never criticizes—even when you typed a wrong deadline on the schedule of an important new book last year and threw production off by two weeks. Some bosses might have yelled. Not him. He understands the pressures you work under and appreciates your skill in coordinating procedures.

Yet when you told him you wanted to apply for an opening in subsidiary rights, his reaction was anything but supportive. "You mean you're going to leave me?" he asked incredulously. "After all I've done for you? Why, subsidiary rights is a tough area. People won't look after you the way I've done. You're too nice for subsidiary rights. Believe me! I know what's best for you. Besides, I need you here with me. You're indispensable."

As we've done with the previous office games, let's look at some of the potential moves. By now you probably have begun to recognize patterns.

If you are making the losing moves, you might:

- Shrug and forget about your career hopes.
- Accuse your boss of being selfish or of suffocating you.
- Agree that it probably is too cutthroat in other departments and add that you feel comfortable with the very professional and rewarding work relationship that you enjoy with him.
- Feel flattered and thank your boss for valuing your work.
- Say he knows best.

If you are making the winning moves, you might:

• Thank your boss for valuing your work, but say it's time for you to move on and develop other skills.
• Tell him that you appreciate the support, but you are ready to try new situations and new challenges.
• Assure your boss you will not leave him in the lurch. Offer to help train your replacement.
• Tell him you believe you can be of more value to the firm in subsidiary rights.

What price do you pay for "protection"? Have you ever analyzed the pitfalls of being told you are "indispensable"? Are you so indispensable that your boss is unwilling to let you go—in effect, standing in the way of your career development?

We're asking, really, whether you are playing Daddy's (or Mommy's) Little Girl. The forces at work here can keep you locked into a lowly place on the office totem pole by praising or cajoling you into a totally subservient role.

The Security Blanket. A job is no rose garden. It's work. If you're in the right job, the work is challenging and rewarding. If you meet the challenges successfully, you grow on the job. But you cannot grow on the job unless there are challenges. A boss who eliminates them is not helping you.

Some of these challenges may involve the "dangers" of life in an organization: personality conflicts, performance and achievement pressure, the threat of job loss. Tucking you under a security blanket to hide those dangers from you can mean that your boss's blanket will smother your professional growth.

Helplessness. Secretaries often cling to a myth of helplessness, a myth shared, unfortunately, by a large portion of women workers. They appear unable—or unwilling—to see their competence and appreciate their near-heroic ability to impose order upon the chaos of office life.

And there are bosses around who help women perpetuate this myth of helplessness. These are the bosses who are all too willing to tuck you under their security blanket.

Loyalty to the Boss. Both you and your boss get rewards from playing Daddy's Little Girl. You get protection and support. He gets your undisputed loyalty. He also gets ego satisfaction: after all, you are "his girl".

Loyalty is fine; in fact, it is a virtue. It stops being a virtue, however, when it is clearly contrary to your self-interest. And it is contrary to your self-interest when you owe your primary loyalty to your boss—at your own expense or even at the expense of the organization. Staying on a job too long because your boss finds you "indispensable" is contrary to your self-interest.

The Praise Trap. It is also against your self-interest to get caught in the praise trap, a frequent snare. Secretaries who fall into this trap receive overabundant praise for both difficult jobs and minor ones. The important point is that it comes frequently and is a sign of constant approval.

Just as children get unconditional love and approval from parents, here the secretary gets what amounts to unconditional and nonstop praise. The danger is that reliance on that daily "fix" of easy praise can keep you in a job you have outgrown. The praise trap kills independence.

The following checklist will help you determine if you're falling into this trap. Which of these attributes does your boss praise?

Ideas
Femininity
Suggestions for new office procedures
Taste in clothes or perfume
Discipline in going for a college degree at night
Loving care of the plants in the office
Determination in planning a rewarding and challenging career
Neat desk
Administrative and coordinating abilities
Choice of gifts for his wife's birthday
Skill in dealing with clients, customers, other employees, management, office systems, etc.
Great coffee
Ambition

Does the checklist point out a pattern in your boss's praise? Is he or she more likely to praise you for comparatively minor skills or characteristics that are irrelevant to the advancement of your career? If so, beware! You may be a victim of the praise trap.

A baby is helpless, an adult is not. The sense of helplessness, however, often persists long after the reality fades.

Growing out of a helpless-protective relationship is not easy. It's not easy for a secretary who has come to rely on a boss's protection. It's not easy for a boss who may be angry with an "ungrateful" secretary if she wants to advance to another position in another department.

But you must persist. Your career, your development as an achieving adult, is at stake. As "nice" as your boss is, as much as your boss wants to "help", you must realize, and get your boss to realize, that this "protection" is hindering your development.

The chances of getting your message through will be better if you relate your needs to the organization's. If your boss is allied with you in terms of your career development, not in terms of "protecting" you, he or she really can be of help.

CLAIMING DUE CREDIT

You are secretary to the manager of the data processing department of a medium-sized insurance company. Business has been superb this year: so good, in fact, that the department cannot handle the heavy load. At the same time, word has come down from the top: no new hires and no new equipment for six months. New office procedures must be devised to handle the work flow.

Your boss, however, is too busy to work on the problem. The bottleneck is getting worse: tempers are frayed, two employees have just quit in disgust, and if more leave the situation could become impossible.

For the next two weeks you don't leave the job when you leave the office at 5 P.M. You find the problem challenging, you know the employees, their abilities and their needs. You want to come up with new procedures that will temporarily solve the work-overload problem.

Your effort pays off. You come up with some good ideas and communicate these to your boss verbally. The boss says, "I'll think about them."

A week later your boss dictates a report. The subject: new office procedures to be in effect for the next six months. The report draws heavily on your ideas. However, you get no credit.

The losing moves in a situation like this might include:

• Sulk because your contribution to the new procedures was not recognized.
• Badmouth your boss for "stealing" your ideas.
• Mentally record that the boss owes you one and hint that you expect to be paid back.
• Gush that your boss was brilliant to think of just the right procedures to see the department through the crunch.

On the other hand, the winning moves might be some combination of the following:

- Say what a good job your boss did in refining your ideas.
- Express pride that your ideas were incorporated into the solution.
- Work hard to make sure the new procedures are effective and then express pride that your ideas contributed to the solution.
- Point out your contribution during your next performance appraisal.
- Make a note of your ''success'' in your ongoing resume (see chapter 11).

The work gets done, the problem is solved, you're all one big team. Does it matter who gets credit for being part of the solution? You bet it does! Several factors are at work here.

Pride.   There is nothing wrong with a healthy expression of pride in oneself and in one's work. In fact, there is a lot *right* about it. Pride should be cultivated, and if your boss doesn't nurture it, you must provide the nourishment. This doesn't mean you should act conceited, but reasonable self-esteem and self-respect require pride in what you do and how well you do it.

Self-Effacement.   That means keeping oneself in the background. Does this attitude describe you? Many secretaries feel most comfortable in the background. Many, however, experience mixed feelings. They don't want to be in an exposed position: that's risky. But they don't want to be ignored either—that could be demeaning.

Today, secretaries are expressing greater unhappiness about being ignored than about being in the limelight. In other words, they want credit. In particular, they want credit for their brains. And they want the opportunity to use them.

We're not talking now simply about credit for the routine elements of the secretarial job. Typing a letter quickly and without errors is important, but it won't promote your career significantly. Superb organizational ability, on the other hand, may.

Rewards.   Reward for achievement is vital for self-respect. We're not talking only of monetary rewards, although money is obviously important. Recognition and status are two other very important acknowledgments of achievement. Often the three go together, but not necessarily. The reward may be money. Or it may be a letter of commendation from the company president. Or it may be a write-up in the company newspaper. Or it may be a promotion, and so on.

You're kidding yourself if you think that recognition means nothing. It's against your own best interest to accept a statement like, "I know those were my ideas in my boss's report, and he knows it, too. That's all that matters". A healthy self-respect requires *open* recognition of your contributions and achievements.

Recognition encourages pride in "ownership", in that you will feel the solution is yours and work all the harder to make it succeed. Recognition also means that you are no longer a replaceable cog in the company machine but a valuable part of its energy, someone who can improve the quality of life at the office. Finally, recognition feeds the ego, which spurs greater achievement, which attracts further recognition and rewards. The result is a dynamic circle of cause and effect—all of which leads to a more satisfying work life.

What kinds of rewards do *you* need? This will depend on your financial situation and your values. You will need to determine for yourself what kind of rewards you need—and then speak up so your boss or others in your organization can meet most or all of those needs.

Claiming due credit shows a healthy sense of self-respect. By taking reasonable credit for your role in coming up with new ideas or new procedures, you reinforce your image as a thinking, creative member of the office team. You are also "buying into" the solution. In effect, you are claiming full or partial "ownership" of the solution. You now have a stake in seeing that the solution works. When it does, don't be bashful about reminding your boss or your personnel department of your contribution.

Remember, if you downplay your role in helping to run an office effectively, others will, too. If you claim reasonable credit, chances are that others will give you that credit.

TAKING CHARGE

You are secretary to a senior vice president. Five junior executives report to your boss and work in the same suite of offices along with their secretaries. Physical proximity has fostered close friendships among the secretaries. All of them have equal status: they function independently and are responsible only to their bosses.

One week your boss gets complaints from several important West Coast clients: phones are sometimes not picked up; often calls are not returned—the assumption is that the bosses never got the messages. Special problems crop up during lunch time, when it is only nine or ten o'clock on the West Coast.

You boss names you "senior secretary" and that afternoon sends out a memo announcing your increased responsibilities and authority. One of your first tasks is to make sure that the phones are covered at all times.

The next day you post a schedule for staggered lunch hours. Later in the week one of the secretaries gets back from lunch a half hour late. The phones were not covered. Your boss is angry.

The following day, another secretary doesn't return from lunch on time. Again no one is there to answer the phones—except you.

The losing moves in this office situation are plentiful:

• Say nothing to the late-returning secretaries, assuring yourself that people will call back if it's important.

• Postpone or eliminate your lunch hour so that you can answer the phones. Perhaps say to the latecomer that you were glad to help.

• Answer the phones yourself and tell the latecomer, in a light and friendly tone, "Well, now you owe me one. Don't worry; I'll collect!"

• Answer the phone yourself and yell at the latecomer, "You've got a hell of a nerve making me miss my lunch hour. Do I have to do everything around here?"

• Threaten to fire any secretary who does not stick to the new schedule.

In looking for a solution that the secretaries will carry out with maximum commitment, you might make these winning moves:

• Meet with the other secretaries as a group to reach a mutually satisfactory solution. This move aims for results not by controlling the other employees but by encouraging them to cooperate with each other and with you.

• Send a memo to your boss outlining the solution agreed on by the team. Ask the boss for comments on the proposed action plan. Sending a memo keeps the boss informed of the situation. It also allows the boss to offer comments on the team's plan.

"Congratulations on your promotion!" is one reaction you may get in your rise to senior secretary. The promotion may also cause resentment and envy, and friendly working relationships may be in for a strain.

Assuming Authority. With the promotion, you have acquired additional responsibility and authority. Your job has changed and it's up to you to work out comfortable and productive new working relationships with the other secretaries. These new relationships represent a shift in power, reflected in the fact that you will be assigning work and enforcing your rules. Assigning tasks to the other secretaries will be inevitable if you and your office are to function efficiently and effectively.

However, don't make the mistake of imposing an authoritarian structure on what had been a fairly loose working environment. Modern management theory suggests that employees who participate in decision-making and problem-solving will be more committed to making those decisions and solutions work. By helping to mold the employees into a team, you help reinforce a sense of team capability, team loyalty, and team pride. Their collective energy and intelligence can be channeled to more than the solution of the immediate problem; it can transform the employees into an effective force for running a highly productive office. And you will have played a pivotal role in the transformation.

Alienation of Co-workers. A potential pitfall when assuming authority over friends or assigning work to them is alienation. They may find the new you to be bossy—not like the old friend who was one of the gang. They may be resentful, jealous, angry, uncooperative.

Don't be surprised—or hurt—by these negative reactions. If you handle the situation with tact and professionalism, you will be able to enlist cooperation, maintain friendship, and perhaps help others to assume more responsibility, too.

If a boss chooses to promote you over your co-workers, tensions between them and you may surface. The group dynamics will undergo change, and change usually brings stress—until a stable, new working pattern evolves.

Don't let the temporary stress keep you from assuming your new responsibilities. Old friendships need not stand in the way; they may, in fact, help you to be more effective in your new job by creating a cooperative environment in which each employee takes more responsibility for his or her work.

Don't fall into the trap of fearing to assign work to a friend. "How can I tell my friend to do anything?" is a reaction that will keep you from enlarging your career horizons.

Moving up may alienate some coworkers. On the other hand, moving up may allow you to help them enlarge their career horizons, too. If you can do it, why can't they? The possibility of upward mobility is an important incentive for working harder, working smarter, working more enthusiastically. And you will have pointed the way.

Chapter Seven

Creative Confrontation

Creative confrontation is an art and as we saw in the chapters on office games, a secretary must learn how to use it.

A confrontation is a face-to-face encounter used to deal with a conflict and with the feelings—especially anger and frustration—created by it. The confrontation, using open and free discussion, allows the principal parties to communicate their basic needs and find a way to satisfy these needs.

A creative confrontation takes place only under certain conditions. If these conditions are present, you will be on the way to a successful resolution of the conflict—then you *and* the other party (or parties) can count yourselves winners.

Careful preparation is always required when you stage a confrontation. This means knowing what your position is and why you have adopted it.

Knowing your mind in advance will enable you to press your case persuasively. As outlined in chapter 5, office situations, especially sticky ones, require you to choose the best of several alternatives after analyzing the pros and cons. Be ready to back your position with concrete details.

You might want to practice stating your position aloud. Keep your presentation simple and brief. Convoluted sentences and thoughts are not persuasive.

Face-to-face confrontation is necessary for a successful conclusion. Memos are good, as we discuss later, but more as preparation or follow-up to the in-person encounter.

Why is the face-to-face element so important? Because it allows communication on many levels—through words, facial expression, body gesture, nuances—and it forces the principal parties to work through their anger, frustation, and confusion together.

No delays: the confrontation should take place as soon as possible after a conflict is recognized. Don't wait until the problem becomes a distant memory. As soon as you acknowledge the conflict, and the usually negative feelings associated with it, arrange for the confrontation. It may take place immediately or at a mutually convenient time for the principals.

If the conflict is with a co-worker, you might want to arrange a lunch date. If it is with a boss, you might press for a free spot on her or his calendar—either that day or the next. Try not to delay the confrontation more than forty-eight hours. Delay weakens the sense of urgency. More important, it generally weakens your will to resolve the conflict.

But, you may be asking, wouldn't a delay allow passions to cool and perhaps avoid a hot-tempered exchange that is rarely productive? We believe confrontations can be staged without delay *and* without rancor: you *can* have one without the other. The hostility caused by flying off the handle with a boss, co-worker, or subordinate can poison any working relationship.

A private setting should be arranged for a confrontation. One staged in a public arena can turn into a circus—and the principal parties, you included, will look like clowns. Take special pains to avoid embarrassing someone publicly—a public loss of face results in enemies, not victories.

A statement such as, "But I did exactly what you told me to do" shouted at a boss in front of other employees is hardly likely to win the boss's favor—especially if you did do exactly as you were told.

Involvement of all the principal parties is a prerequisite. If you are arranging the confrontation, it's up to you to determine who these are. Sometimes this is tricky.

For example, the conflict in chapter 5 over the marketing VP's request for a temp involved the secretary, the VP, the boss, and the controller. For the secretary, however, the conflict was really over the clarification of her authority: the principal parties were the secretary and the boss.

In other situations, the confrontation may involve several persons. For instance:

The receptionist at one company developed a serious but temporary illness. She would be out of the office for at least a month. Betsy, the secretary to the firm's president, had to arrange for the other secretaries to handle the receptionist's duties. She devised a schedule that divided the receptionist's duties equally among all the secretaries.

Problems cropped up very soon. One secretary forgot she had to cover the phones on Tuesday and again on Thursday. Another came back late from her lunch, and Betsy had to postpone her own lunch date to cover the phones. Still another secretary complained that the workload was already too heavy.

This was clearly a conflict situation. All of the secretaries were participants; and all had to be in on the confrontation.

The resolution was simple and straightforward. Betsy called the secretaries together. "We have a problem," she said. "Let's get together this afternoon to decide how to handle it. Any problems with four o'clock?" There were no problems with the time. They met and worked out mutually convenient arrangements. The phones were covered and the receptionist's other duties were distributed among the secretaries whose work loads were lightest.

This situation was an example of employees solving their own problems rather than waiting for direction from above. The secretary who fosters this type of cooperative environment, in which employees take on additional responsibility and work to their fullest potential, stands out as eminently promotable.

Persistence is needed if you want to be successful in a confrontation. Don't be ashamed to repeat yourself: repetition drives your point home. In a conflict situation, it's unrealistic to expect somone else to support your view simply because you offer it once or even a couple of times. Essentially, you are selling the other party on your point of view.

Persistence must be practiced at virtually every stage of a confrontation, even in arranging for the encounter. Imagine, for example, that your boss says she has no time to talk to you about your complaint that you lack authority to handle a problem.

YOU: I don't have the authority to handle the problem on my own. I'd like to talk to you today about getting more formal authority.

BOSS: Sure, I want to talk to you, too, but I have no time today. You know how busy my schedule is.

YOU: Yes, I know how busy you are. But it's important that we talk. You told me to handle this new problem but I don't have authority to act on my own. And I run into a lot of

situations like this. The problem is serious for our department.

BOSS: Oh, it's not all that serious. We'll talk when I can catch a
            minute.

YOU: The problem *is* serious. Things come up which I could
            handle if I had more authority. But I don't. I'm caught in
            between. I can help you in situations like this, and then
            you'd be free to concentrate on the bigger problems. I'd
            like to schedule a fifteen-minute appointment with you
            tomorrow.

BOSS: I wish I had fifteen minutes to give you. You know how
            busy I am.

YOU: I know you're busy, and that's part of the problem. Our
            work gets bogged down, and things don't get done. You
            have fifteen minutes free first thing in the morning. Let's
            schedule our talk then.

BOSS: Maybe you *will* be able to help me more. Okay, tomor-
            row, first thing.

A workable compromise is just as essential as persistence in successful confrontations. Suppose your boss insists that she cannot
squeeze in a fifteen-minute appointment with you for the following
day. Your persistence runs up against her persistence. Then it's time
for a workable compromise. Both of you share a similar overall objective: to make sure that the office functions effectively. Beyond
that, however, your aim is to arrange a meeting with her as early as
possible; her aim is to meet with you when she has the time.

    Let's replay the end of this dialogue:

YOU: You have fifteen minutes free first thing in the morning.
            Let's schedule our talk then.

BOSS: Tomorrow is out of the question. I'll be preparing for a
            9:30 meeting with Frank Gray. No, I'm sorry, we'll have
            to postpone our little talk until next week.

YOU: It's very important for our department—and for me—that
            we resolve this issue as soon as possible. Your schedule on
            the next morning is lighter. Let's arrange for our talk at
            9:00 o'clock Wednesday.

BOSS: Well. . .

YOU: Jill, you know I wouldn't press you on this if I did not con-
            sider it very important.

BOSS: I'll tell you what. I'll come in the next day fifteen minutes early. We'll meet at 8:45. Can you get to work a little early that day?

YOU: It's a deal! I'll be here.

Practice makes perfect; confrontations get easier the more you engage in them. If you find them difficult—perhaps they're not your "style"—don't give up. On the contrary, seek out opportunities to practice. Only with experience will you learn how to handle confrontation comfortably.

Follow up: a confrontation is truly successful only if the gains last. Too often they don't. Why? Often because there is failure to follow up.

Systems seem to have a life of their own. Changes decided on in a confrontation may be implemented for a short time. A couple of months later, though, things have slipped back to where they were before. Follow-up can help. Simply note on your calendar when you should reexamine the situation to make sure that the gains are still in place—and working. The frequency of the follow-up should depend on the importance and complexity of the problem. The point is, don't work out changes and then simply assume that everything is going to be fine.

Think of the follow-up as your personal tickler system. You follow up on things for your boss. Now follow up on an encounter for yourself.

USING MEMOS IN CREATIVE CONFRONTATION

Creative confrontation is not easy. A lot of work goes into it. A lot of courage and imagination go into finding new ways to resolve the conflict. Many methods and tools can help along the way. Memos are one such tool. They can precede the face-to-face encounter, or they can follow up on decisions made during it.

Secretaries tend to shy away from sending their own memos, either because they are too busy typing their boss's memos or because they don't feel confident that their opinion warrants a memo.

Don't believe it! Memos are a valuable tool for secretaries—especially if used sparingly. Think of the pluses in it for you:

• Memos force you to think about a problem—and often, to think creatively about it.

• Sending a memo enhances your visibility. Your boss, and perhaps others, will know that you care enough about the problem to spend time thinking about it and communicate your ideas.

• Since higher-level employees are usually the ones to write the memos, the fact that you would do likewise lends you an air of professionalism.

• Memos are documentation. Your contriubtions are put on the record.

But beware! Don't overdo it. Your boss probably already has an overload of paperwork, and an avalanche of memos won't be appreciated. Save the memos for your most important information or ideas.

What's in a Memo?

Suppose there is a conflict among secretaries over use of the word processor. Suppose further that you want to suggest holding a group meeting to resolve the problem. Does your boss want to read a fully detailed account—an analysis to end all analysis? Certainly not. Your boss does not have the time and might not even have the interest. So what *does* your boss want? A memo that is brief and contains only the essential facts.

How to choose the essential facts? Judgment. *Your* judgment. You choose the facts you consider essential, based on first-hand knowledge of the situation. You, or your co-workers, know which facts are essential because they involve you. They involve your work situation.

What belongs in the memo?

A brief description of the problem and its consequences. What is the problem and how does it affect you, your boss, your co-workers, the organization? For example, do you and other secretaries have to wait too long to use the word processor? How does this affect your work?

Your recommendations. Try to suggest a solution, or even a set of options. A call for a meeting of departmental secretaries is one option.

What doesn't belong in the memo?

Interesting, gossipy tidbits. Your boss wants to read the memo as quickly as possible. She's not reading it for entertainment!

Analysis of facts about which you have little or no knowledge. For example, leave it to the controller to give detailed memos on the cost/benefit considerations of a new word processor.

SAMPLE MEMO

To: Barbara Cane
From: Lois Caplan
Date: January 5, 1983
Re: Word processor tie-up
Problem: The secretaries in our department have trouble
             getting to use the word processor. We share the
             equipment with Registration and there are too
             many of us for one machine. We all need to use
             it, and we waste time waiting in line. Some of us
             have had arguments about who should use it
             next, whose work is top priority and should be
             done first.
Recommendation:
             Call a joint meeting of our department and
             theirs. You and the Registration department
             head can be there along with all of the secretaries
             who use the word processor. The purpose of the
             meeting would be to work out an effective system
             for using the machine.

How to Write A Memo

You don't have to be a Shakespeare to write an effective memo.
Just keep it simple. Stick to the point. Don't go overboard with the
language: fancy words are out of place in a business memo.

The easiest way to write a memo, at least at first, is to say it
aloud. What are the facts? What's the problem? What's your recommendation? Use words that would be natural if you were speaking to
your boss. Then type out your message. Read it over. Is it simple? Is
it brief? Is it clear? Edit it to make it simpler, briefer, clearer. Then
hand it in. Don't stew over each word. Don't try to make it perfect.
If you've gotten your message across, the memo has achieved its
purpose.

Once you've handed in the memo, don't forget about it.
Follow-through is essential; it should come no later than a day after
you handed in the memo. Since you write memos only for important
matters, it is important that you get a speedy response—and natural
that you should press for one.

The follow-through should be face-to-face. It can be brief. Simply ask if your boss has had a chance to read your memo and say you'd like to talk about it. Try to arrange for a private talk immediately or set a mutually convenient time within the next twenty-four hours.

Be persistent in following through. Don't let a busy boss try to confuse persistence with pestiness. You are *not* being a pest when you identify a problem, send a memo on it, then press for feedback. If you cared enough about the problem to write a memo, it's only natural that you want to know what action your boss will take.

Since memos are so important in creative confrontation as well as in general problem solving, it pays to master the technique. Your boss can provide valuable feedback at first on the memo itself, as well as the problem outlined in the memo. Find out if you included all the information needed to understand the situation. Get suggestions: "Did I describe the problem clearly? Was there enough detail? Too much detail? Did my recommendation make sense? Was the language I used easy to understand?" This will enable you to improve each succeeding memo. And you'll feel more comfortable each time you hand one in.

The secretary has two very important advantages in writing memos to her boss: daily contact with the boss and knowledge of the boss's schedule.

You can use these advantages. Other employees, even those with managerial status, don't have the power—yes, the power—of arranging the boss's schedule to fit in a period of uninterrupted talk. Use this power discreetly, but use it! Use it to make your confrontations productive and creative.

Mastering the art of creative confrontation takes years. Some people may never really feel comfortable with it, but they learn from each new one. Those who can wield confrontation as a savvy tool on the job acquire a sense of independence: they are in control of their professional lives. And, paradoxically, with this sense of independence often comes the strength to collaborate freely with others at all levels in the organization. Knowing you will not let yourself be dominated will free you to seek cooperative working patterns. With today's emphasis on team effort and collaborative rather than authoritarian work environments, creative confrontation is not merely a good idea: it is a necessity.

Chapter Eight

Daring to Dream

So far we have been looking at the objective realities of your work life—the skills you practice on the job and the interpersonal skills needed to move ahead. The skills inventory helped you to identify your on-the-job skills; the office games illustrated the interpersonal skills essential for career movement, growth, and self-fulfillment. Now you know what you can do, but do you know what you want to do? And how can you spark the internal boost necessary for the next stage of career development—making career dreams come true.

It's time to leave the path of objective reality to explore your deepest emotional hopes for a career, and tap the energy of those hopes. It is this energy that gives you the will to change and creates the commitment necessary to see you through the arduous path of career advancement. Forget who you are, what you can do, what you must do. It's time to let yourself go and fantasize about what you really *want* to do.

CONSTRUCTIVE FANTASY

"I've never been able to let myself think the sky's the limit," Ann was telling the seminar when she found herself having trouble fantasizing about her job. "I'm just too unimaginative—or practical."

Karen Metzger, a psychologist in New York City, finds that Ann's reaction is not unusual. "When I ask secretaries to tell me their fantasy jobs," she says, "most don't give an outrageous answer. Often, their fantasy jobs are well within the bounds of possibility. But they don't allow themselves to explore their options—no matter how realistic they may be."

Fantasy is a mind-opener. It is an extremely useful and practical technique in career planning. It is particularly useful if you have not allowed yourself to explore the full range of your options. Earlier we recommended fantasy as a method to allow you to see skills that you could value if only they were part of your "ideal" job. The fantasy was a technique to help you envision those skills as transferable.

Fantasy has other purposes as well. It helps people to identify their interests. Fantasizing about an ideal job helps to pinpoint vague, unrealistic, impractical, pie-in-the-sky aspirations that, on further examination, may not be so impractical or pie-in-the-sky. It also functions as your personal spark plug by giving greater reality to those vague dreams and propelling you toward the steps that will make those dreams come true. Sound impossible, even ridiculous? Not at all! Fantasy is a very powerful thinking tool, and we're going to show you how to use it to your benefit.

HOW TO SPARK THE FANTASY

Fantasizing about jobs may be difficult at first. You, like Ann, may never have let yourself think that the sky's the limit. Secretaries, in particular, are often shy about fantasizing. But fantasies can be sparked.

To fantasize most productively, you must be comfortable and relaxed and provide yourself with sources of inspiration. Most important, ask yourself the right questions. You can't ask, "What do I want to do for the rest of my life?" warns psychologist Karen Metzger. "That's too big a question." Narrow it down, though, and you can come up with creative, workable fantasies that highlight major interests. Visualizing specific aspects of a job can often achieve that narrower focus. Ask yourself questions to fill in the details.

Find a position that helps you fantasize. Sometimes an ordinary upright position—sitting or standing—can inhibit fantasies. In other words, upright can be uptight. Lying on your back may allow you to relax enough to give way to the fantasy. (Lying down, however, may have just the opposite effect: a supine position makes some people feel vulnerable, and they just won't allow themselves to give in to the fantasy.) Choose the position (or place) that works for you.

Leaf through magazines. Get your ideas, and sparks, from as many sources as possible. Magazines are one such source—and a rich one at that. Articles and ads can spark images of an environment you want to work in and the people you want to work with.

Visualize your ideal work environment.
• Is the setting indoors or out?

- Do you have your own office?
- How large is the room you are working in?
- Are there drapes?
- Is there a desk? What is on it? Is there more than one desk in the room?
- Is there a bookcase? What types of books are on the shelves?
- What's on the walls?
- What type of equipment is in the setting?

- *Visualize the other people on the job.*
- Are they customers? Clients? co-workers? Subordinates? a boss?
- What do the others look like?
- How are they dressed?
- What expression is on their faces? Pain? Happiness? Fear? Anger? Respect?

- *Visualize the activities you are performing.*
- Is money being exchanged?
- Is there a product?
- Are you writing? talking? reading? selling? thinking?
- Are you helping other people?

Try another fantasy. You're not limited to just one fantasy. A second or even third job fantasy offers valuable clues in career planning. Perhaps eventually you'll combine elements from two or three fantasies to come up with a tailor-made job to aim for.

Allowing yourself more than one fantasy has another important advantage. The first is often far-out. Then comes the thought: but *this is what I* really *want to do.* And this second fantasy job, while still exciting, is often much more realistic.

Experiment with group fantasy. If you're still having trouble, maybe you need other people to spark the fantasy. A group will come up with questions you probably would never have thought of on your own. Other people provide different points of view. They expand horizons. They trigger thoughts. They stimulate. They challenge. They encourage.

And they can make the fantasy experience fun.

How do you find such a group? Establish a network of colleagues, as we suggested earlier. Begin with your friends; many are probably secretaries. Invite those both on the job and off to explore with you the potential of group fantasy. Initially, keep the group restricted to secretaries. They probably have had similar work experience to yours, and this may make the fantasizing easier.

However, some of your friends are probably *not* secretaries. Ask them to join the group after the first session. People with other work experience can expand the fantasy horizons for you and the other secretaries in your network.

HOW TO WORK WITH THE FANTASY

Now it's time to put your fantasy job skills inventory from chapter 2 to use, or to do another skills inventory if you have changed your fantasy. What skills do you use in your fantasy job? These match your deepest-felt fantasy interests.

Do you have those skills? Do you use them on your current job? Have you used them in previous jobs? Do you use them in hobbies? Do you use them in connection with family-related activities? How do they match up with the skills highlighted in your regular skills inventory?

Consider Marilyn's fantasy job. Marilyn has always dreamed of being a big-time baseball coach. She laughed as she confessed her lifelong fantasy. The closest she had gotten to her dream job is to coach for Little League in her leisure time. "I love that coaching," she told the seminar. "And you know, I'm good at it. I can see the difference I make in the kid's playing. Why even some of the fathers tell me how much I've improved their kids' game."

Before you dismiss Marilyn's fantasy job as ridiculous, read on. Marilyn is a secretary in the personnel department of her company. Besides her typing, steno, and other routine secretarial responsibilities, she conducts initial job interviews and explains personnel policy to employees. Her regular skills inventory identified strong interpersonal skills, which included communication, instruction, policy interpretation, tact; capacity to perceive needs and skills of others, to make realistic demands of them, and to motivate them. Those were the skills she wanted to use more of, and her fantasy skills inventory confirmed this. She realized that she liked to help people grow.

Marilyn's company had not yet begun any serious employee training and development, an area that could dovetail with her love of coaching. She could try to expand the training and development policy in her company—and that component of her job. Marilyn was ideally situated for that exploration. She was in the right department!

What about Ann, who had such trouble fantasizing about an ideal job? Like Marilyn's, her dream job can be used to generate creative career plans. Her fantasy is to be general manager for a crafts business. Needlepoint is her passionate hobby: she designs her own work and helps friends with theirs. Her hobby requires attention to detail with perception of overall design. Ann is a secretary in a small savings and loan association (SLA). Her regular skills inventory identified higher-level business skills: decision-making, problem-solving, planning, coordination, and information organization and analysis. She likes to use those skills and wants to develop them further. She now sees the potential learning advantages of working in an SLA: she can learn about fundamental business realities—particularly financing—while she expands her business skills and begins seriously exploring and pinpointing her career path. She is now thinking of returning to college for a degree in business management, which would help her turn her fantasy into reality.

What if there's a mismatch? Suppose the skills in your fantasy job bear little relation to your experience? If you have come up with a mismatch, try another job fantasy. Put yourself in another job environment. Go through the same process of filling in the details: What people are involved? What activities? Is there a match this time?

If there's still no match, analyze whether you can acquire the necessary skills. For example, Ann realized that she would need a business degree in order to become the general manager in her fantasy job. If your fantasy job is really an impossible dream, try to salvage as many aspects of it as possible and use those to explore realistic job objectives. This exploration is the next stage of your career planning, and it involves extensive research.

Fantasy is a powerful tool but a dangerous one if you don't test it against reality. It's important not to demand too much of fantasy: it does not pick your career, nor does it find you the right job. Fantasy is simply a very useful and enjoyable technique to help you identify your strongest interests and point you toward areas that you would like to work in. Then it's up to you to explore these interests, make a career decision, and follow through with the practical strategies described in the remainder of this book—strategies that can turn your dreams into reality.

NONCAREER SATISFACTION

Before going on to the research tasks in career planning, there is one other important application of job fantasy. Just because the fantasy involved a job does not mean you need apply the identified interest *only* to a job.

You can gain satisfaction from those interests through a hobby or through volunteer work, for example. In other words, you don't have to be a ballet dancer to love ballet. Taking ballet classes or buying a season ticket to the ballet may do the trick.

While indulging in your fantasies in this nonprofessional capacity, you will be enriching your life while pursuing a different sort of career for which you *do* have the required skills. Remember: although your career is an important part of your life, it is not your *whole* life—and your total life satisfaction certainly is not limited to what you do between 9 and 5, five days a week.

Chapter Nine

Research and Networking

Jane is thirty years old. For the past year and a half she has worked as the secretary for two men in her high-tech company: the advertising manager and the purchasing manager. She became a secretary after taking a six-month intensive executive secretary "entree program" at a secretarial school. Before that she taught reading at the elementary school level. She is a college grad, with a degree in education.

Jane's interests are varied. She is artistic: abstract painting is one of her hobbies. She is athletic: tennis is another hobby. She loves the theater: she has attended acting workshops and performed in amateur productions.

Jane's career objectives? She hasn't a clue. Jane is burdened by an embarrassment of riches: good education, talent, work experience as a teacher and a secretary, and well-developed hobbies from which she has gained experience and skills. Jane wants to find a satisfying career. She has a lot of work ahead of her, but she has a lot to work with.

Jane is at an early exploratory stage. She has identified three fields that might offer her a satisfying career: advertising, where she could use her artistic talent; training and development, where she can use her teaching, acting, and artistic skills; and purchasing, where she can use the ordering experience she acquired as secretary to the purchasing manager.

Where does Jane go from here?

To the library. And to people. Jane must learn about the fields in which she has interest and skills. She has to explore what's out there. She has to do the preliminary research that will allow her to ask intelligent questions so she can determine which is the field for her, research that will both broaden her scope and pinpoint specifics. Only then can she make an intelligent career decision.

Too many secretaries at this stage don't give themselves the time to explore in depth the many possibilities open to them. Instead, they use a shotgun approach—aim their sights all over the field and achieve only hit-or-miss effectiveness. If they do bag a job, it may well be another secretarial job, and often not one that offers challenge and growth potential.

It's important not to skimp on this stage of career planning. Don't refine your goals too quickly. Give yourself time to explore a field—to read the right books, skim the right magazines, see the right people, ask the right questions. Inevitably, of course, some of the books, magazines, people, and questions will be *wrong*. No matter. That's why you need the time—to learn which are the right resources for you and what are the most appropriate questions at this point.

Before you start, set a deadline for exploration. We recommend six months. By setting a deadline, you won't run the risk of letting this stage drag on unproductively, a growing danger, you will find, as you get more and more involved in what's out there. While you do not want to refine your goals too quickly, you also do not want to fritter away your time on useless research. Although you may not know at the beginning what is useless, you will get a sense of this as you go along.

There are times when you may feel pressed to speed the exploratory research. Say you have just been laid off. Your landlord won't wait until you have found a job that meshes your skills and interests. In that situation, temporary secretarial work may be the answer—it will pay the rent while you continue to research career options. Or you can take a job to hold you over while you go on with your research.

If you are not in your desired career slot, you should be looking for it. The search may be more intensive at some times than at others. But the search should go on.

In fact the search should go on even if you are *in* your desired career slot. Don't wait until you're out of a job before resuming your research. Chances are that you will then grab whatever is available, not what is best for you. Continue your research; be aware of the job market; cultivate contacts that may lead you to an even better job.

Ongoing career planning is not a sign of disloyalty. It is a sign of a serious career professional who is looking for jobs that will best use his or her skills and interests. And the best way to begin that planning is to visit the library.

USING THE LIBRARY

Many people are intimidated by libraries. Before rejecting the library out of hand, however, give it another chance. It is an invaluable resource, especially since you will not be able to afford all of the books needed in your exploratory research. Besides, this is not an assignment a teacher has given you; it's one you've given yourself. Try it! You may even like it!

The important thing is to find a library you are comfortable in—a community college library, a public library, or a special interest library (such as the library for Catalyst, a nationwide nonprofit organization where women can get guidance in their career choice).

Once you've chosen the library, get the librarian on your side. Explain your purpose. Ask for help in finding the vocational guidance resources and how to use them. Librarians have chosen their career because they enjoy helping people. They want to help you. Let them!

Where to start your career research? If the task of career planning seems monumental at this stage, don't despair. You have already identified your skills. And you have identified your interests. Those were the beginning steps. Your task now is to relate your skills and interests to an appropriate occupation.

Books and other printed material can help. We will recommend those we believe are the most useful in getting you started. You'll find your own favorites along the way. That's the joy of searching for information. It's really a big treasure hunt.

Three books are basic to your library research. These are the *Guide for Occupational Exploration*, *The Dictionary of Occupational Titles* (fourth edition), and the *Occupational Outlook Handbook*. All are published by the federal government. Just ask for them by name in the library.

Designed by the U.S. Employment Service, the *Guide for Occupational Exploration* is an excellent place to start. It is a first step in exploring a potential new career. The information provided is very basic; the guide is intended for people who may not even know what questions to ask to determine if a field is right for them. It asks the questions, gives the answers, and leads you to the next stage in your research. The language is simple and nontechnical; the organization is relatively straightforward, giving numerically-coded titles and job descriptions by area of interest. The *Guide* will help broaden your scope. For example, if you have identified good written and verbal skills, have a strong interest in communications, and are considering being a writer-editor, you will find listed such job titles as newspaper editors, publishing editors, broadcast editors, technical editors, and so on. Perhaps the most valuable assistance offered by this book is the questions and answers that help you to clarify whether a field corresponds to your skills and interests and whether you want to explore it further.

Your preliminary career research has now brought you to the imposing *Dictionary of Occupational Titles*, or the *DOT* as it's commonly referred to. This volume, with its twenty thousand job titles, will give you further descriptions of jobs that you have identified as closest to your skills and interests. Don't be put off by the sheer volume of the *DOT*. Use it as you would a dictionary, only here you are seeking the exact duties that make up the definition of a job. The job titles are listed in numerical order by a nine-digit code number, which corresponds to those given after each listing in the *Guide for Occupational Exploration*. Since the *DOT* might at first confuse you, take time to browse through it at the library. If you are having trouble, ask the librarian for help in learning how to find the items yourself. It's all part of the treasure hunt.

Here is a sample *DOT* listing:

132.267-014 EDITORIAL ASSISTANT (print. & pub.)
associated editor; assistant editor.

Prepares written material for publication, performing any combination of the following duties: Reads copy to detect errors in spelling, punctuation, and syntax. Verifies facts, dates, and statistics, using standard reference sources. Rewrites or modifies copy to conform to publication's style and editorial policy and marks copy for typesetter, using standard symbols to indicate how type should be set. Reads galley and page proofs to detect errors and indicates corrections, using standard proofreading symbols. May confer with authors regarding changes made to manuscript. May select and crop photographs and illustrative materials to conform to space and subject matter requirements. May prepare page layouts to position and space articles and illustrations. May write or rewrite headlines, captions, columns, articles, and stories according to publication requirements. May initiate or reply to correspondence regarding material published or being considered for publication. May read and evaluate submitted manuscripts and be designated MANUSCRIPT READER (print. & pub.). May be designated according to type of publication worked on as COPY READER (print. & pub.) when working on newspaper and COPY READER, BOOK (print. & pub.) when working on books.

The Department of Labor's *Occupational Outlook Handbook* is very simple to use and valuable for long-range planning. Once you have identified possible occupations, you want to know if there is going to be much employment opportunity in them. The handbook gives the most current and comprehensive information available on work to-day and job prospects for tomorrow in several hundred occupations and thirty-five industries. Included is information on the nature of work, working conditions, training required, places for employment training, employment outlook, earnings, advancement possibilities, related occupations, and sources of additional information. It's useful to get clues on what government experts anticipate will be the job outlook for an occupation or industry even if, as Richard Bolles advises in his excellent book, *What Color Is Your Parachute?*, intelligent job hunters can find jobs where they are told none exist. Better to get the information, then disregard it if you choose.

From these three books, you can identify job titles and lay the groundwork for your understanding of occupations and industries. Once you choose specific careers about which you need more information, it's time to intensify your research.

Every library has one or more series of career guidance booklets. One set is probably just as good as the other. Ask the librarian for help in finding them. If your library has no career guidance booklets on hand, ask the librarian to order a set. We recommend three, but if your library does not stock these, the series it has on hand is probably equally good.

The "Vocational Guidance manuals," published by Career Horizons, are extensive and worthwhile. Among more than eighty books in the "Opportunities In" series are those that highlight advertising, banking, broadcasting, public relations, magazine publishing, sales and marketing, paralegal careers, hotel and motel management, and recreation and leisure. Easy to read, each booklet describes the work, education and experience requirements, earnings, and working conditions in the industry.

Career Horizons has also begun a new series entitled "Women In." Five books have appeared thus far, focusing on women in communications, engineering, finance, management, science, and entrepreneurial business.

Catalyst, the national network of career resource centers for women, has published the "Catalyst Career Opportunity" Series. These booklets offer career options for women who have a college degree or are planning to get one. Accounting, public relations, and advertising are among the fields highlighted.

After identifying those careers that interest you the most, it is time to "get out in the field." In other words, it's time to talk to people, which experts agree is the most effective way to research a job. However, even after starting your people research, don't abandon the library completely. Continue to use the librarian to help you probe. As you do more research, your questions to the librarian will get more precise and productive—neither too specific nor too general. The upshot: better research.

There are many reference works that will upgrade the quality of your research. They will lead you to other publications as you begin to focus more narrowly on a field. The *Directory of Professional and Trade Organizations* lists names and addresses of groups to which you can write for printed literature. *Books in Print* lists all the books published recently, organized by subject, author, and title; the subject listing will allow you to find books according to occupational topic.

Periodicals guides—especially the *Readers Guide to Periodical Literature*, the *New York Times Index*, and the *Wall Street Journal Index*, which are all standard resources—enable you to research past and current literature in magazines and newspapers. This is your best way to keep up to date on recent developments in your field of interest.

One other resource is Ulrich's *Directory of International Publications*, which lists the names of all journals and magazines, arranged according to subject area. Ulrich's includes listings of trade and professional periodicals, some of which you should check out to see if the material really does interest you. Ask someone in the field that interests you to recommend one or two of their leading professional or trade magazines.

Of course, once you find the listings, it's up to you to follow through. Your library will probably contain many of the books and periodicals you seek. Ask the librarian how you can get those not available at the library you're using. Most libraries participate in interlibrary loan services and provide the means to get copies of periodical articles.

It's also a good idea to get in the habit of reading at least one of the major business publications regularly, especially if you are seeking employment in private industry. Choose from among *Business Week*, *Industry Week*, *Fortune*, *U.S. News and World Report*, *Inc.*, *Forbes*, and the *Wall Street Journal*.

Keep up to date on developments in your area by reading the local newspaper, especially the business pages. Don't skip articles that might provide job hunting clues, such as the opening of a new business, the transfer of a company headquarters into your city, the growth or decline of an industry in your region, and so on. Change is all around you. Cast a wide net to keep you in touch with what is happening.

Do as much research as you can. The more you know about a field or an organization, the better your people research will be.

GETTING INFORMATION FROM PEOPLE

People are your most valuable source of information during the occupational research stage. A personal interview is a form of reality testing—you can find out what you can *really* expect from the job.

People with successful careers can give you specifics that books rarely reveal: how they got started and moved up, what are the usual entry-level job titles and career paths in the field, how you can plan your career path. Equally important, these people do not simply provide information; they are valuable contacts for the future. But make very clear that at this point you are looking for information, not employment.

Making Contacts

Finding people to interview is the first step after you've narrowed the field in the library. The best way to find contacts is to let people lead you to other people.

You may be surprised by whom you know. Or whom you know who knows a person you want to see. Or whom you know who knows a person who knows a person . . . you get the idea.

Send out word to everyone that you are doing career research. Make it clear that you want to talk to people in the fields that interest you—to get information, not a job.

Which people can help at this stage? Your friends. Your relatives. Casual or not-so-casual acquaintances. Neighborhood folk (your cleaner, hairdresser, butcher, or dentist). All of these people know other people. By working through them, you will vastly expand your range of contacts. And these people will generally be delighted to help. It's a boost to the ego to be the one to put you in touch with a person who can help you.

But what if you strike out? What if you can't get a personal referral? The phone can help you out. Simply call a business and get the name of the person or persons employed in the field you are researching.

Say you are interested in fashion merchandising. Call a department store in your city and ask for the name of the fashion director.

Then call the fashion department and ask for that person *by name*. You may reach the fashion director's secretary, but that should not be a great problem: you are a pro at talking to secretaries when you place calls for your boss. Tell her, in your most professional manner, who you are and, in a sentence or two, why you're calling. ("Hello, this is Anne Winston. I'm researching employment opportunities in fashion merchandising, and wanted to get the fashion director's point of view. May I speak to Alison Sloane?") Sometimes the hardest part of getting through to VIP-types is getting up the courage and self-confidence to make the call.

If you cannot get through to the person you want to see, explain what you're doing in greater detail to the secretary and ask her for suggestions on whom to call. Tell the secretary that she can be very helpful in your research by providing names of contacts. Everybody likes to think that she or he knows the key people. Most are willing to pass on this information. It makes them feel important!

Names of people are all around you. Open your daily newspaper, turn on a local TV show. There are people in those stories. They may be people who are in the field or job you want to know about. Get the names from the stories and then get in touch.

Use your imagination in gathering names. For example, suppose you want to explore career opportunities in the nonprofit world and a local newspaper has just reported that the director of a day-care center has received a United Way grant. Give the director a call and try to set up an appointment. You might say that you saw the announcement in the paper, congratulate her for getting the grant, and then say she would be an ideal person to give you information about work in a nonprofit organization. A bold move, true, but it just might catch the person's interest.

If it doesn't work, what have you lost? Some of your efforts to reach people will pan out. Others will not. The more methods you use, the more people—and wider range of people—you will reach.

Use a contact to get to other contacts. At the end of an interview or phone conversation, ask the contact to suggest other people whom you can call or write. Ask whether you can use your contacts' names. Chances are they will say yes. After all, you are, in effect, saying that their name means something to the person you want to reach. The underlying message: you appreciate that they know the "right" people.

Think of your contacts as part of a giant chain. One person is linked to another who is linked to another, and so on. You want to connect with that chain—and eventually become a link yourself. That's how the system works—through people. If you understand that simple, basic principle, others will think you know not only who's who but also what's what.

Setting Up an Interview

Let's say that you have made phone contact with the person you want to interview. What do you do now?

• DO be direct. And DO be brief. Say clearly and concisely what the purpose of your call is.
• DO make it clear that you are doing career research, not asking for a job.
• DO be specific about the amount of time the interview will require.
• DO be prepared. Know what you will say. Practice it alone or with friends. This is particularly important if you are shy about acting on your own behalf.
• DON'T act shocked that VIP Alison Sloane is willing to talk on the phone with little, insignificant you. She, too, was once just starting out in the field.
• DON'T grovel. Alison Sloane is a busy woman, and you shouldn't waste valuable time telling her over and over how wonderful she is to talk to you.

Once you get through to your contact, setting up the actual interview should go something like this: "Hello, this is Anne Winston. I would like to interview you about the field of public relations. Chuck Grant suggested you would be just the right person to give me information to help in my career research. I could get by with as little as fifteen minutes of your time, and of course, we could arrange the meeting *at your convenience.*"

Note three things in setting up the interview:

• Use the word "interview" right up front. A flattering buzz word, it will massage the egos of the prospective interviewees and will reassure them that you don't intend to pester them for a job.
• Mention the name of the person who referred you. Although undoubtedly you mentioned the name to the secretary, repeat it to the prospective interviewee. The name means something to the person, so use it.
• Tell the person how much time you need. The best approach is to mention a minimum time and add that, of course, you would appreciate even more if it's available.

If the person is just too busy now, try to arrange for an interview at a later date. If that doesn't work, ask the contact for the name of someone else to interview. Be persistent, but also be polite and professional. The contact may simply be too swamped with work at the present time or may be going out of town or may have dozens of other perfectly valid reasons for not seeing you. However, you may be referred to an assistant, to a colleague at another company, or to someone else who can supply you with worthwhile information.

One last consideration before we get to the interview itself. If you are a student, communicate the fact up front. In fact, a student doing school research may have an edge in getting interviews. Even very busy people seem open to students wanting to learn about their profession.

Making the Interview Productive

An interview is divided into three parts: before, during, and after. This is true for *any* type of interview. Each part requires different action.

BEFORE
- Prepare at least six to eight questions in advance. Preparation is important to avoid wasting the interviewee's time—and yours.
- Plan on a fifteen-minute interview, especially if you specified fifteen minutes when you requested the meeting. Keeping this time frame in mind will force you to focus on the vital issues during the planning stage.
- Set a priority for the questions. Decide in advance on a logical order of progression (usually from the general to the specific works well), and on the order of importance. This will be the order to follow during the interview.

DURING
- Take notes or use a tape recorder. However, check first that the interviewee will feel comfortable with the method you choose. The advantage of a tape recorder is that you will miss nothing. You will be able to replay the interview when you are not under pressure. Important pieces of information will, therefore, not slip by unnoticed. A recorder will also allow you to focus all of your attention on what the person is saying. You won't have to worry about whether you're getting it all down. If you choose to take notes, make them as brief as possible. Don't spend the whole time scribbling. Use shorthand, but don't use a steno pad. You don't want to reinforce your

image as a secretary. The notebook should be small; in it will go names of people, places, and other vital information.

• Listen carefully to the responses. Active listening—really hearing what the other person says—will heighten your spontaneity. You want to pick up on points that are of greatest interest to you. But, you may ask, how can I balance preparation with spontaneity? Preparation actually allows for *more* spontaneity. Because you know what questions you need answered, you will know what information is important. When unexpected points arise during the interview, you can junk the prepared questions for spontaneous ones because you will recognize that these are even more central to your concerns.

• Ask open-ended questions—those beginning with what, where, when, why, and how. Questions requiring yes or no answers will usually not tell you much. On the other hand, questions such as the following could unlock riches of information: What is the best way to get into your field? What new job possibilities are available at my level? What are standard career advancement moves? What interim career moves did you make and what jobs did you hold that led to your current position? If you had the budget to hire an assistant, what would you most need that assistant to help you with and what skills or experience would you look for? What do you like best about your job? What do you like least about it? What are its greatest satisfactions? What skills do you absolutely need for your job? What talents or personal attributes are most needed in this field in general, and specifically at this company?

• At the end of the interview, ask for referrals to other people. This is *very* important. Don't forget the chain system. Sometimes a job offer may result from the career research interview. Congratulations! But don't accept it, at least not immediately. Tell the person you will consider the offer but are not ready to make a decision. Research is a very important stage in career planning. Don't cut it short by grabbing the first job offered—or even the second or third. Of course, if the job offer comes at the end of the research stage and the offer is what you are looking for, you may want to accept it. But give yourself at least twenty-four hours before making a commitment.

AFTER

• Write down your impressions of the interview, and of the job described, immediately after the meeting. Did you feel that the person seemed less happy with the job than he or she said. Did you sense that the person was encouraging or discouraging your pursuit of that field? Are you more, or less, interested in pursuing the field further?

• Analyze the information obtained in the interview. Evaluate how the job description dovetails with your skills and interests. Did you get the information you wanted? (Your questions will change as you get a more realistic idea of what the jobs consist of. They will become more targeted, perhaps more detailed, as you acquire more information.)

• Send a thank you to the interviewee. The note can be extremely brief. Offer your services to the other person, if appropriate.

Researching careers through libraries and people will provide you with the most precise, concrete, practical information you can get to make a career choice. Research is challenging. It can even be fun—once you get the hang of it. And you will get the hang of it as you acquire experience in career research.

Don't expect to master the library or be an experienced interviewer the very first time. You will acquire the experience, and the expertise, with each new reference source you use and with each additional interview.

At some point you will realize that you're not learning anything substantially new in the interviews, that you can anticipate what the interviewee will say, that you have heard enough. We can't say when this will happen—you must be the judge. But then it's time to take the plunge: it's time to make your career decision.

Chapter Ten

Your Career Decision

Nancy, a secretary who embarked on career research, completed her exploratory work in about four months. During this time, she:

- talked to many people about different types of jobs
- identified communication skills as her best skills
- heard many people say how good she was at selling herself
- took an adult education course in sales and sales promotion to learn what the field was all about
- read books, trade magazine articles, and other material pertaining to sales
- talked to her uncle's friend, a sales manager at Philip Morris, and to that company's director of executive development
- read a book on sales as a profession and took a seminar recommended by her uncle's friend

She also thought long and hard about why, after six years, she no longer wanted to be a secretary and found she:

- was tired of being in an office from 9 to 5
- wanted to be out in "the big world"
- wanted to control her life and her job (she had come to feel that a secretary is controlled by others on the job)
- wanted to make more money than she knew was possible at the top secretarial salary range
- felt that secretarial work did not utilize all her skills and talents

In other words, Nancy did a lot of soul-searching to clarify her values and needs. She decided on her life-style priorities, set her financial goals, and made clear to herself the sort of working environment she wanted.

Nancy's excellent communication skills, experience in dealing with people, and desires to work in a less structured environment, to be "more in control," and eventually to make more money were pointing her in the direction of a sales career. Her book and people research along with the clarification of her values and needs reinforced her growing interest in this field.

Nancy was ready to make a career decision. Her overall objective: media sales. Her short-range goal: get a first job in sales. The latter was important for two reasons: she needed actual sales experience, and she needed to get rid of the secretarial title.

But some of you will reach a very different and unexpected decision: you will discover that the secretarial profession is right for you. Jodie has found this to be true for many secretaries who began her seminars with only one goal in mind: not to be a secretary.

Sue, a secretary for ten years, verbalized her self-discovery this way: "I didn't realize before that there were so many aspects about being a secretary that I really liked. But after listening to the other secretaries in the workshop, I could see this clearly. And I could also see that, with the help of a supportive boss, I could bring about changes in a job to make it more challenging and fulfilling, more in line with what I'm looking for in my work."

Sue went on to enumerate what she liked about being a secretary:

- She liked the variety of responsibilities.
- She liked dealing with many different kinds of people.
- She liked, and was good at, making things run smoothly in the office.
- She liked, and was good at, organizing time, setting priorities, and meeting deadlines.
- She liked being close to the seat of power and acting as a sounding board.

After much soul-searching and researching of alternatives, Sue reached her career decision: to grow and develop within the secretarial profession.

Let's say you have spent six months exploring career development possibilities. You have done a thorough skills analysis, you have identified your key interests, you have clarified your needs and values, you have pored through vocational guidance and specific career books, you have talked to many people in the occupations that most interest you, and you have thought carefully about why and in what way those occupations interest you.

Having done all that, you are ready to make your decision. There are four aspects to this decision; we call them the Four Musts. The Four Musts of a career decision are:

It *Must* be your own.
It *Must* be written down.
It *Must* be realistic and attainable.
It *Must* include a specific time frame.

It Must Be Your Own.   Your boss might have ideas for your career. So might your spouse, or your friends, or your mother or father, or your teachers, or your carreer counselor. The ideas are theirs, but the career is yours. The decision is yours.

To be committed to the decision, you must feel that you ''own'' it, that you have a stake in it. This sense of ownership is very important—it allows you to feel in control of your career and helps mobilize the energy needed to succeed in it.

It Must Be Written Down.   Get your decision down on paper. You'd be surprised at how much more real the decision becomes when you write it down. It also becomes workable, because you have boiled down your interests, skills, and fantasies to a concrete goal. You have set a target. Now you can take aim.

Your written career decision must be a succinct statement. It is the end result of your months of exploring, thinking, analyzing, refining. The language must be specific, positive, and strong. You are beyond the fantasy stage. You don't just ''want'' to be something; your goal is to be in a very definite job. The statement should indicate the scope of the responsibilities you seek.

Nancy's career decision statement might have read: ''My long-term objective is to be a member of a large sales staff for a TV network.''

Your career decision statement is for you. It sets your target. It reminds you of what you will be working toward. Once the statement is written down, refer to it often: it will reinforce your determination to achieve it.

It Must Be Realistic and Attainable.   Is making a realistic and attainable career decision easier said than done? Not really! As you know, having spent six months identifying your skills, exploring your career objectives, and writing down your decision. It is easy to say and do now because you have put in the hard work to reach the decision.

To reinforce your decision and to help make it attainable, break it down into achievable goals—long-term, intermediate, and short-term. For example, Nancy's long-term goal was to be in media sales. Her short-term goal was to get a first job in sales.

A realistic and attainable career decision will ultimately require a detailed schedule of steps that must be taken as part of a career action plan. At this point you need write down only the first two steps. Make sure the first steps are easily attainable—it's important to guarantee success so you will be encouraged to proceed.

Nancy's first two steps were to prepare a resume and then to send her resume, along with a cover letter, to companies placing help-wanted ads in the local newspaper.

Note that Nancy's first step was not to get a job—this might not be easily attainable. But she could successfully prepare her resume, and she could send the resume to companies running help-wanted ads. When she completed the steps, she checked them off on paper. Seeing those check marks gave positive reinforcement to her fledgling action plan—and to her overall career decision. She was on her way.

You might argue that she stacked the deck. What's the big deal in preparing a resume and in answering help-wanted ads? Anybody can do that! Precisely! Anyone *can* do it, but Nancy *did* do it! It's all right to stack the deck. Just make sure you stack it in your favor. And then feel proud that you succeeded in that step.

Constantly seek ways to make the career advancement process easier. Don't erect unnecessary obstacles. It's a difficult process. Since you are doing it by yourself and for yourself, set it up so you can see yourself making progress.

After checking off the first two steps, write down the rest of the steps that will lead on your short-term goal. Nancy, for example, arranged and went on job interviews. Achievement of the short-term goal completes stage one of the overall career action plan.

Once you have attained your short-term goal, draw up a step-by-step career action plan that will get you to your intermediate goal. When you have achieved that, continue the plan all the way down the pike—to your long-range objective.

Along the way, you may revise your action plan. This is no big problem—as long as the changes ease the process. Thinking in terms of short, separate steps will ensure that your career decision is realistic—and attainable.

It Must Include a Specific Time Frame. When you set your short-term, intermediate, and long-term goals, establish specific time targets. But understand the purpose of these targets. They are there to guide you along the way to success, not to bind you to a rigid schedule that is a constant source of anxiety. The purpose of a time frame is not to set deadlines for failure, but guideposts for progress. If after six months you haven't gone on any job interviews, ask yourself if you've worked at it hard enough, or been realistic enough in your expectations.

The time frame must be realistic. Don't expect to achieve your long-term goal in three to six months. On the other hand, don't allot ten years' time to achieve a short-term goal!

Long-term goals are where you want to get to. They may take five years, perhaps ten or fifteen. Your research and your starting point will determine how much time to set. Intermediate and short-term goals are your way stations, the stopping places en route to the final destination. These goals allow you to pace yourself: you don't want to burn out along the way.

Use specific time targets for the steps necessary to achieve short-term goals. These interim activities are the most achievable and, therefore, the most controllable.

Let's say your long-term goal is to be a fashion buyer for a large department store. Set up your career action plan along these lines:

> Long-term goal: To be fashion buyer in lg. dept. store
> Time: 3-5 years
> Intermediate goal: To get job as, or be promoted to,
> ass't buyer
> Time: 1-2 years
> Short-term goal: To get job as sec'y. to merchandising mgr.
> Time: 3-6 months

The stage during which you work toward the short-term goal is the period for finding your career-positioning job. This stage is very important since you can't move ahead with your career plan if you accept just any job. It is essential to place yourself in a spot where you can get the experience and, perhaps, the promotion possibilities to move toward your intermediate and, eventually, long-term goals.

The interim steps toward the short-term goal may occur simultaneously. In the future fashion buyer's case, they include:

- Prepare resume (includes printing): 8 days
- Prepare cover letter: 2 days
- Get names of contacts in fashion merchandising: 4-8 weeks

- Send resume and letter to specific merchandise managers: 4-6 weeks
  - Set up job interviews: 4-8 weeks
  - Go on interviews: 4-8 weeks

The most important information to get on your interviews is whether a secretary can become an assistant buyer in that store. Does the store have a management training program in which a secretary can prepare for the assistant buyer's job? What can you learn on the job to help you gain the necessary experience to be an assistant buyer? Does the prospective boss seem supportive of your career goals?

Once you have achieved your short-term goal, you begin work on the steps leading to your intermediate goal. This stage involves a saturation learning process. In effect, you are qualifying yourself for your next target position. For example, you would need to learn about the company (procedures, aims, staff, problems, and how they all fit together), make contacts, explore the competition, read the professional literature, promote yourself among colleagues and superiors, and, in many cases, obtain outside education.

Let's say that you have obtained your short-term goal: secretary to the merchandising manager. Now your activities would be geared toward getting the assistant buyer's position. During the one to two years you've set aside to achieve this, you would:

- Take fashion merchandising courses at a local college.
- Learn departmental merchandise for each buyer's department, names of manufacturers, selling procedures in each department, retail terminology, paperwork procedures, fashion trends, and display techniques.
- Keep your eyes and ears open around the store for possible openings as assistant buyer.
- Research the competition (comparison shopping).
- Read *Women's Wear Daily*, *Vogue*, *Bazaar*, and the style section of your newspaper.
- Tell your boss, personnel department, friends, and acquaintances that your long-term goal is to be a fashion buyer.

Setting short-term, intermediate, and long-term goals allows you to plan your career development realistically. Targeted goals that are your own, that are written down, that are realistic and attainable, and that fit within a specific time frame—these are the components of an effective career decision.

Along the way, you will acquire deeper self-knowledge and self-appreciation that will advance your effectiveness, not only in your career but in every aspect of your life. The result: an image not as *just* a secretary but as a top-flight professional in whatever career track you choose.

Chapter Eleven

Resumes and Cover Letters

Resumes are *not* a vital factor in getting a job. In fact, the resume can't get you a job. But it *can* get you an interview for a job. And "the object of any written documents—resume and correspondence—is to get the interview," says Carol Cox, senior vice president of personnel and communications at an international research and marketing organization.

If prepared and used correctly, the resume is a powerful tool in your career advancement campaign. That doesn't mean you can't advance without a good resume; it simply means it helps. And you should use every tool and technique at your disposal to promote your career.

The resume enhances your image as a professional. Indeed, the resume is a standard tool of the job-seeking professional—whether manager, engineer, computer programer, chief executive officer, or secretary. It is your record of professionalism—past and future. The resume describes not simply your jobs—present and past, secretarial and nonsecretarial—but your effectiveness on those jobs. It achieves this by describing your accomplishments and the skills you use—skills that you can transfer to your target job.

The resume helps you organize the facts so that you and your prospective employer can see them clearly. Summarizing your skills and accomplishments, and highlighting those most relevant to your objective, gives you and the prospective boss a concise wrap-up of who you are professionally—what you've done and what you can do.

There are no rigid rules for preparing a resume, but there are general guidelines. It's then up to you to decide what to put in and where—and your choice should be governed by what will best promote your career objective.

Your resume should be no longer than one page. You must assume that the person reading it is busy; a three-page resume takes too much time to read. A long resume does not mean a more impressive job history, nor a more impressive person. It does mean that the person has not taken the time to think through his or her accomplishments and highlight them for the convenience of the person with the power to hire. The most effective resume communicates distilled excellence. It entices the prospective employer to want to know more about the person. After all, the prize for a good resume is an interview with the prospective employer. The details left out of the resume can be filled in during the interview.

The resume should be straightforward. The prospective employer "wants the facts, ma'm, just the facts." "What really turns me off," says Robert Surles, director of executive development at Air France, "are cutesy gimmicks. When I see a resume typed on colored paper or accompanied by colored folders or when I see photos attached, I can't help thinking that there's less here than meets the eye." He sees these as evasive techniques designed to camouflage the real person. "I want to see clearly what the person did and where," he explains.

A well-organized resume gets your message across quickly and clearly. It tells the reader what you can do and what you want to do. Because it is an organizing tool, it shows the reader how well you can organize information.

HOW TO ORGANIZE YOUR RESUME

Each resume begins with the same introductory basics. Then comes your career objective. What comes next depends on your choice of format: the chronological or the functional. We will describe both. Education and other information appear where they will do the most good.

Begin with your name, address, and telephone numbers (business and home) at the top. Placement depends on your aesthetic preference as well as the amount of available space. (For some ideas, see our sample resumes later in the chapter.) Do *not* include such information as your birth date, marital status, or other personal information. Myrna once received a resume from a college professor who wanted to write for her journal. His resume included his wedding anniversary and the birthdays of his two children. This did attract Myrna's attention—but only to the inclusion of information she found bizarre and *not* to his qualifications for writing for the journal!

Writing your career objective or goal should not be difficult at this point, since you have already worked out your career decision and career decision action plan. The career objective on the resume should capsulize in one or two lines your career decision action plan, picking up on the beginning (the type of job you are looking for today) and the end (where you are headed).

If you keep in mind the purpose of the resume—to get an interview for a career-positioning job—then your strategy becomes obvious: to be specific enough to set you on your chosen course but not so specific you limit your opportunities. The career objective must alert the prospective employer to the type of job you are looking for immediately—the target area and entry level. It must not be too narrow, since an overly specific objective can limit the chances of getting your foot in the door. At the same time, your objective must not be too broad, since you have done a lot of self-analysis and career research in order to land a job that sets you on your chosen career path.

Different situations will require somewhat different degrees of specificity. For instance, if you are a secretary who wants to make a career switch, eventually working in media sales, your resume career objective would read: "A position in sales with advancement opportunity." Because your aim is to get your foot in the door at any level, and get rid of the secretarial title, you must be vague about the initial position and also about the area of sales in which you want to work.

However, if you are the secretary to a merchandise manager of the dress division in a department store, and you want to get rid of the secretarial title (and ultimately become a fashion buyer), your career objective might state: "Merchandising position that could lead to a career in fashion buying." Here, you are vague about the exact position since several jobs—fashion coordinator, department manager, or assistant buyer—would set you on the appropriate career track.

Or say you are secretary to the director of a nonprofit organization and want to get into fashion merchandising, but you lack experience in this area. Your career objective in this case would read: "Secretary in a retail environment where I can learn the basics of fashion merchandising." Since you are using your secretarial skills to move into another industry in order to gain the knowledge and experience needed to advance within that industry, you need to be very job specific while leaving your long-term goals more vague.

From here on, the organization of your resume may vary according to your needs and circumstances. The two most effective resumes for the secretary are arranged according to chronology or function. Whichever you choose, it should highlight your skills and accomplishments on the job, as well as the results for the organization. The chronological and functional resumes have different formats; and each has its strengths. It's up to you to decide which is the best for you.

Chronological Resume

The chronological format, which stresses job titles and organizations, is particularly good if your work history is specifically related to your career objective. The chronological resume could get you an interview if:

• You want to make a lateral move—for example, from one secretarial position to the same job in a different company.
• You want a higher level job but still want to remain in the same field—for example, if you are now a secretary and want to be an executive secretary.
• Your job history shows progressive growth and you want to take a further step up the organizational ladder—for example, if you've worked your way up to senior secretary in your division and now want to be an office manager.
• If your company is prestigious and your position gained you experience directly related to your career objective—for example, if you have been secretary to the sales manager of a very respected company and now seek an entry-level position in sales. (The functional resume may work here, too.)
• Your job history shows a series of jobs that gave you substantial knowledge of the field in which you seek a nonsecretarial job—for example, if you've held several secretarial posts in the purchasing division, and now wish to position yourself for your long-term goal of purchasing manager with a *Fortune* 500 company. Your short-term goal might be to secure a job as assistant purchasing manager in a large company or as purchasing manager in a small company. (The functional resume may work here, too.)

Your employment history begins with your present job and goes back chronologically. If you have had many jobs, emphasize those that support your career objective—no more than four. Either list your other jobs, or combine them. Do not cover in detail more than the last ten years.

For each job, select the accomplishments and responsibilities that most strongly support your career objective. Don't list everything—minor accomplishments will be assumed. For example, if you organized your boss's filing system, you need not include the filing of daily correspondence. Focus on results and use action verbs to describe them. Be specific. Look at the difference between, ''My duties included purchasing office furniture" and "Purchased equipment and furniture valued at $500,000 for new office," or between, "My duties involved filing" and "Organized new filing procedures for personnel records."

As these examples illustrate, it is better not to use full sentences or the word "I." A telegraphic style—action verb and result—saves space, focuses on concrete action, and tells the prospective boss that you don't waste time and space on nonessentials.

Use separate lines for each accomplishment. Bullets, dashes, or asterisks lend emphasis. You may prefer to describe your duties in a short paragraph—still using phrases rather than sentences. This style is acceptable, but we find the other easier to read. List the accomplishments in order of priority. Don't list more than five accomplishments for any one job.

Functional Resume

The functional format highlights your strongest skills and accomplishments, those that relate directly to your career objective. The functional resume could get you the coveted interview if:

• You have been on the same secretarial job at the same company for a long time and now want to change careers by drawing on skills acquired on the job—for example, if you have acquired many public relations skills as a secretary and now seek a nonsecretarial position in PR.

• You have had several short job hops, acquired substantial experience in certain skills, and wish to capitalize on these skills for a career change—for example, if you have worked with word processing in a few jobs and now want to be a marketing support representative in word processing.

• You are returning to the job market and want to use skills acquired since you left the work force—for example, if you left a secretarial job seven years earlier in order to raise your children and now want to draw on volunteer and family experience to get a job as a conference coordinator. In this situation, your work history fails to reflect your growth and your competence; a functional resume could capture both.

The focus of the functional resume is the listing of major skills that make your career objective reasonable. Your skills inventory will help you pinpoint your most important and most used skills. Choose three to five skill groups that are most important to your career objective. Examples of functional, or skill, headings include:

Interpersonal, Administrative, Financial, Writing, Research, Training, Coordination, Public Relations, and Organizing. Some of these headings may overlap. Choose the ones that best describe your skills and accomplishments.

List the skill areas in order of importance to your career objective. In each area, list your accomplishments, again in order of importance. Do not list more than five accomplishments under each skill. This forces you to select the most important ones. Include any relevant result or accomplishment without identifying where you achieved it. Nonpaid work accomplishments should be included. Focus on results, use action verbs to describe them, and use a separate line for each accomplishment. The suggestion made earlier—action verb and result, in telegraphic style—applies here, too.

A synopsis of your work experience, arranged as a list, can go either before or after your skills, depending on how recent the jobs are. If you are now working, or have had a job within the last three years, it is better to list the experience above the skills. This allows the reader to see the work context in which you acquired the skills. If you have been absent from the work force for a period of time, give the work synopsis at the end of the resume.

Which format to choose, you ask, chronological or functional? There is no one answer for every individual and every situation. Experiment. Try the resume in both formats, and see which one presents your strengths in a way that will get you the interviews.

While many prospective employers seem to prefer the chronological resume at least initially, others, when they see what we mean by the skills resume, are equally impressed. The format you choose is primarily dependent on your background, skills, and goals.

The education section requires a flexible approach. What to include and where to place it depends on your particular circumstances. If you are a college graduate, list your degree, where and when you received it, and your major. Then list other courses and seminars related to your career objective. Begin with the most recent ones and then go backward. Also cite courses in secretarial training. Don't bother mentioning your high school graduation.

If you are not a college grad, list in reverse chronological order any courses and seminars related to your career objective. If you spent some time at college but did not get a degree, list the name of the college, the dates of attendance, and major courses. If you are currently a part-time college student, begin with that information, giving the college where enrolled, your anticipated degree and when you expect to receive it, and your major.

Should secretaries without a college degree cite their high school graduation? We advise against it. Individuals who have taken, or are now taking, college courses and even secretaries without any college experience should not mention their high school degree. Today it adds nothing to your credentials. In fact, there is an automatic assumption that a secretary is a high school graduate. Besides, you will probably be asked this information on any job application forms.

The placement of educational information within your resume depends on where it will do the most good. That depends largely on how relevant the educational credits are to your career objective and how recently you obtained them. We recommend you list you educational history after your work experience unless, of course, your educational background is more impressive than your employment. You may want to cite educational credits first if you have little job experience, if your education is directly related to your career objective and your jobs are not, if you graduated recently, if you attended a highly prestigious college, or if you achieved academic honors.

The one-page space limitation will determine how much other information to include. Here, as elsewhere in the preparation of a resume, you must use judgment. Determine how relevant your other interests are to your career objective—and how helpful they are to your image.

Do not include such interests or special talents as skydiving, dancing, and tennis, unless they are related to your job objective. However, do include such information as fluency in languages, published works, community service related to your career objective, and membership in professional organizations. Myrna has seen one resume that lists languages this way: French, COBOL, and Pascal (the last two are computer languages).

The heading you use depends on what information you are offering. It can be general (Miscellaneous, Special Interests, Special Activities, Awards) or specific (Languages, Published Works, Professional Memberships).

The following checklist provides some dos and don'ts for presenting your resume:

Use an 8½" x 11" sheet of white paper.
Put name, address, home and business phone numbers at top.
Use 3/4" margins on all sides.
Single space items; double space between paragraphs.

Use captial letters and underlining to highlight important information.
Use bullets or asterisks to separate and highlight information on individual lines.
Be generous with white space.
Be neat: a sloppy resume makes a very bad impression.
Do *not* include marital status.
Do *not* include birth date.
Do *not* attach photos.
Do *not* draw designs on the resume.
Do *not* mention that references are available on request.

THE ONGOING RESUME

The resume, to repeat, does not get you a job: it gets you an interview for a job. Does that mean that once you get the job, you don't need more interviews, and therefore don't need more resumes? No!

The resume is an extremely useful tool in the ongoing process of your professional growth. Working on the resume throughout your career, even when you're not looking for a job, enables you to keep track of your accomplishments. The ongoing resume is not for a prospective boss. It is not for a personnel director. It is for you. Experiment with it. Play with it. Watch it grow. And watch yourself grow, too.

If you record your achievements in your ongoing resume, you will not be stymied when you need to recall them to look for a job—and must update your resume. Set aside a regular time to update your resume. What did you do? What were the results for your organization? Be specific.

It is not necessary to record *everything* you did. Record only those tasks that were important for the organization. Concentrate on decision-making, problem-solving, communication, and organization—key areas to your advancement.

The resume is your tracking tool. It is also your goal to further achievement. If several months pass without an addition, ask yourself why. What can you do worth recording on the resume?

COVER LETTERS

If the purpose of the resume is to get an interview, the purpose of the cover letter is to get the employer to *read* the resume. Cover letters should accompany every resume sent out.

SAMPLE CHRONOLOGICAL RESUME

Nancy A. Blake   27 Ashland Avenue
                        Glen Rock, NJ 07452
                        (201) 472-1544(H)
                        (201) 256-8200 (B)

CAREER GOAL: Sales Representative with opportunity
                 for advancement and travel.

WORK EXPERIENCE

1979-   Secretary to President, S.B. Thomas, Inc.

. Compute daily and monthly sales figures for report
   to Board of Directors.
. Prepare and research goals presentation for Board
   of Directors.
. Responsible for renewals and payments of contracts.
. Facilitate communication between president and subordinates.
. Report on activities for company newspaper.

1977-1979   Secretary to National Sales Manager, Panasonic

. Acted as liaison between National Sales Manager and
   field representatives.
. Arranged local and national sales meetings.
. Interviewed, hired and trained new office employees.
. Assisted Japanese executives adjusting to U.S.

1976-1977   Secretary to President, Costa Development Corp.

. Maintained daily records of sales and rentals of townhouses.
. Prepared confidential company information for lending
   institutions.
. Opened new office in Florida.
. Responsible for communication between Florida and New Jersey
   offices.

EDUCATION

Current   Thomas A. Edison College, Associate in Arts
                 (June 1985 graduation)

   1981 Dale Carnegie Course in Effective Speaking and Human Relations
   1979 Selling and Sales Promotion
   1978 Katharine Gibbs Course in Modern Management

AWARDS AND COMMUNITY SERVICE

. Human Relations and Achievement Awards, Dale Carnegie
. Member, Board of Recreation, Ridgefield Park, N.J.
. County Committeewoman, Bergen County, N.J.

SAMPLE FUNCTIONAL RESUME

Nancy A. Blake
27 Ashland Avenue
Glen Rock, NJ 07452

Bus. Tel. (201) 256-8200   Home Tel. (201) 472-1544

CAREER GOAL: A position in sales with opportunity for
                 advancement and travel.

SPECIAL SKILLS

Interpersonal
. Facilitated communication between president and
  subordinates
. Acted as liaison between National Sales Manager and
  sales representatives
. Assisted Japanese executives adjusting to U.S.

Administrative
. Prepared and researched goals presentations for Board
  of Directors
. Interviewed, hired, and supervised new office employees
. Opened new office for land developer in Florida

Financial
. Computed daily and monthly sales figures for report
  to the Board of Directors
. Responsible for renewals and payments of contracts
. Prepared and administered budgets for numerous
  volunteer organizations

WORK EXPERIENCE

1979-   Executive Secretary to President, S.B. Thomas, Inc.
1977-79   Executive Secretary to National Sales Manager,
             Panasonic
1976-77   Secretary to President, Costa Development Corp.
1973-76   Owner-Manager, Dairy Queen

EDUCATION

Current   A.A. program, Thomas A. Edison College
             (June 1985 graduation)
1981   Dale Carnegie Course in Effective Speaking
             and Human Relations
1979   Course in Selling and Sales Promotion
1978   Katharine Gibbs Course in Modern Management

AWARDS AND COMMUNITY SERVICE

. Human Relations and Achievement Awards, Dale Carnegie
. Member, Board of Recreation, Ridgefield Park, N.J.
. County Committeewoman, Bergen County, N.J.

Carol Cox, senior vice president of personnel and communications at an international research and marketing organization, considers the cover letter "critical". She is disposed to find a resume more interesting if the cover letter is interesting, she confesses. In fact, if the cover letter grabs her interest, she may want to see the person even if the applicant does not meet all the qualifications of the job.

Remember, the personnel director looks at hundreds of resumes. A cover letter that promises an interview with an interesting applicant is more likely to obtain an interview. And if the interview is good, the personnel director may tailor a position to fit the person. Hiring is not all that cut and dry!

Cover letters are important whether you want to remain a secretary or want to change careers. Use the decision to be a secretary as a selling point. You might say, "I enjoy being a secretary and want to remain within the secretarial profession, but I want a more challenging job." Cover letters are particularly important for secretaries who want to change careers, but for a different reason. They offer more flexibility than resumes for stating why you are qualified for the job and for a career change. These rules will help you to write a winning cover letter:

• Be brief. The cover letter should be no more than a page. Again, entice the reader quickly—assume that he or she is busy.

• Address a specific person whenever possible. Only when answering a blind newspaper ad will this not work. In all other situations, a little phone research will do the trick. Simply call the organization and ask for the name of the person in a specific position—for example, the director of fashion merchandising. Single out an individual at the appropriate organizational level—a manager or vice president. The trick is to get to someone with authority, but not someone responsible for the whole organization—unless, of course, the organization is very small.

• In the opening paragraph say something personal that shows you know something about the company. Then state how you would like to fit into that organization. Tailor your career objective to the needs of the organization. For example: "I was delighted to read in the *Journal Courier* that you and your partner had purchased Radio Station WRAN. I would welcome the opportunity to be part of your sales staff."

• Indicate how your experience and skills can be of value to the employer—for example, mention your contacts with the business community.

SAMPLE COVER LETTER

27 Ashland Avenue
Glen Rock, NJ 07452

February 8, 1983

Robert Sillerman
Radio Station WRAN
Randolph, NJ 07844

Dear Mr. Sillerman:

I was delighted to read in the Journal Courier that
you and your partner had purchased Radio Station
WRAN. I would welcome the opportunity to be part of
your sales staff.

I have lived and worked in this area for the last
eight years and have been very active in the
community as county committeewoman. My job and
community experience have allowed me to meet and work
with many levels of the business sector.

I would like to meet with you at your convenience to
discuss the possibility of a job at Radio Station
WRAN. I shall call next week to set up an
appointment.

Sincerely,

Nancy Blake

- Ask for an interview. Suggest a date and time: "I am planning to take vacation time the week of May 11 and would like to meet you then at your convenience." This gives you a good opening for a follow-up call to set a date. Even if you do not suggest a date, say you will call soon to arrange a meeting. This is important. Do *not* say that you hope to hear from the person in the near future—a vague statement at best. You'll get better results by taking the next action yourself. You may get rebuffed, of course. But you may get an interview. And that's what you're after.

The resume and cover letter are tools of the professional. Both are geared to get you the interview that can get you the job that advances your career.

By now you have put a lot of work into exploring and focusing your potential: you know your skills, you appreciate them, you have chosen your career objective, you have taken steps to strengthen your image, you have learned to communicate effectively. You are ready to find the job that moves you toward your career objective. Interviews are the next step—a career objective interview with your current employer or a job interview with a prospective boss.

Chapter Twelve

Moving Up in the Same Company

Monique had been a secretary in the North American division of Air France for twelve years. First she was secretary to the reservations and ticketing manager and then secretary to the general manager, who became vice president of the North American division.

Monique was slow to leave the secretarial track, having enjoyed the protection of her boss and the feeling of indispensability to him. But gradually she felt the need to switch. She started focusing and preparing herself for a move. Sales and marketing were the areas she targeted. She decided to stay at Air France for another year. During that time she would learn as much as possible from her current job and would take on more responsibility. She also would let Air France know that she wanted to move ahead in her career.

She scheduled a meeting with Robert Surles, the director of executive development. She loved her job, she told him, but wanted to move on to a "commercial job", something in marketing or sales. "I'm ready," she announced.

Surles was impressed. "Monique was very well prepared," he recalls. "She said, 'this is what I can do, this is what I've been exposed to, and this is what I need. How can Air France help'?"

Surles recommended a course in international marketing and another in career opportunities for women. The airline would pay. Moreover, he promised to notify her of any potential openings in marketing or sales. During the last week of her marketing course, the position of reservations manager opened. She asked for an interview and got the job. She now supervises a staff of twenty.

Why did Monique get the managerial position? One factor was the career objective interview: Surles saw evidence of Monique's self-assurance, self-knowledge, maturity, and good organization. Because of the interview, and also because of his awareness of her excellent performance on the job, he knew she could make decisions under pressure, was willing and able to solve job-related problems, possessed superb organizational skills, and had good interpersonal relations with co-workers, bosses, and customers.

In short, Monique used a career objective interview to full advantage—and it paid off.

THE CAREER OBJECTIVE INTERVIEW

What is a career objective interview? To understand that, we need first to examine what it is not.

A career objective meeting is not offhand. It is scheduled in advance—and you come prepared. You determine beforehand what points you want to make, and you are persistent in making them. If you seek answers to questions, you persist in getting those answers.

"I don't want to be a secretary anymore. Do you have any ideas?" The major shortcoming in this approach is that the secretary has failed to project an image of someone who knows her worth and can suggest areas for growth potential. She seems unwilling to take responsibility for her own career.

"Sharon in the MIS department, has just been promoted to administrative assistant. That's what I'd like to be. Why was *she* promoted and I wasn't?" This time the secretary has stated what she'd like to be (administrative assistant) and has invited more information (why Sharon was promoted and she wasn't). But this secretary deflected the focus of her remarks away from herself to Sharon. Moreover, she began the question with a defensive "why," which often invites a defensive response. The boss may feel obliged to defend the decision to promote Sharon rather than to explain what this secretary can do to become an administrative assistant.

The career objective interview is not offhand, does not burden the boss with all the responsibility for devising creative ideas, does not focus on someone else, and does not put the boss on the defensive.

A career objective interview is a formal discussion between you and your boss and/or your personnel department. The purpose is to exchange information: what you can do, what you want to do, how your skills and abilities can be used toward your career objective, what training and other assistance the organization can offer, what advancement possibilities exist within the organization. This information is geared toward achieving maximum growth potential on the job—growth potential geared toward your goals.

The interview makes good common sense: now that you have identified your career objective, see how far you can work toward it in your current job or your current organization. In many cases, your boss or your personnel department has no idea of your career goals. Even is you've told them once or twice, they forget. Tell them again!

The career objective interview, therefore, is a probe: you are determining what kind of mutually beneficial match is possible with your organization.

The initial interview is the most important—and the longest. It should last from thirty minutes to one hour, depending on the amount of ground to be covered. One hour is ideal but tough to get.

This chapter focuses on the initial career objective interview, but if you get satisfaction from the first, there will be more. The follow-up interviews may be considerably shorter—from fifteen to thirty minutes.

If your company has regular performance appraisal interviews, you may want to incorporate the career objective interview in one of them. Both cover a lot of the same ground. Moreover, a merger of the two would allow you unofficially to insert the career objective interview into the organization's established system. Result? The interview would automatically be scheduled at least once a year.

The most important drawback to such an arrangement is the danger that your boss's need to appraise your performance would overwhelm the career objective discussion. How to make sure this doesn't happen? Simply think of the interview as an opportunity not just to hear what your boss requires of you on the job and how he or she evaluates your performance, but also to remind your boss of what skills you have used on the job, what accomplishments you have achieved, and how your skills and experience are transferable to your career objective.

Your initiative is required from the very beginning. Let's say that your boss has just set up an appointment for your performance appraisal interview. It's up to you to extend the scope to meet your needs.

BOSS: Personnel tells me it's time for your performance appraisal, so I guess we might as well get it over with as soon

as possible. Please check my calendar and let me know
when I have a free half hour.

YOU: I'll let you know right away. However, I want to schedule
it for a full hour, since it'll give me a chance to discuss my
career objectives with you. I know you can give me some
good ideas.

By giving advance notice, you ensure that your career objectives will come up during the discussion—whether you or your boss
brings it up.

If your company does not have regular performance appraisal
interviews, it's up to you to arrange a career objective interview.
Bring up the idea with your boss: "I would like to talk to you about
my career objectives and want to arrange a meeting for this. I know
you can give me good ideas."

If your boss agrees, fine. Proceed to the next step—the interview itself. However, beware of the inconclusive "agreement." For
example, your boss might respond, "Sure, nothing I'd like better.
But listen, Pat, this is probably the worst time in the world for me to
squeeze in a little extra time for you. Next week will be better. Remind me then."

Don't push when you first broach the topic. You may have
taken your boss by surprise, and pushing may be preceived as a
threat. It's enough just to raise the issue. However, you now have an
opening to pursue the subject the next week. And you must follow
up! Failure to do so will reduce your credibility: it will seem as
though your weren't serious to begin with.

The next week you must again take the initiative: "I've checked
your calendar for the best time to have my career objective discussion. I can fit in an hour-long meeting on Wednesday at four. If
that's all right with you, I'll go ahead and schedule it."

If your boss agrees, you have won the first important step. If
your boss balks, however—"Gee, Pat, I want to do it but honestly
this week is almost as bad as last. I have so many things on my mind
that I know I won't be able to give you the attention you deserve.
Next week may be better. Remind me then."—the time has come to
persist! You can respond, "Mary, I know how busy you are, but I'd
like to talk to you about my objectives this week. Next week's
schedule won't be any better, and the free hour this week will be
perfect for us to get started. It's very important to me that we have
this talk."

Your boss may now agree to the meeting. Then again, she may
try another way out: "Pat, I know it's important to you, and,
believe me, it's important to me, too. Don't you know that I want to

help you as much as possible? Believe me, next week.'' Don't fall into the guilt trap that this boss has set. These is no reason to feel guilty
about pressing for the meeting. In fact, you *must* press further. And
the way to press is with the core statement: ''I would like to talk to
you about my career objectives.''

''I know how busy you are, Mary, but this talk is extremely important to me. *I would like to talk to you about my career objectives.* If this
week is out of the question, we can set up a meeting for next Tuesday
at three. Is that OK with you?''

Chances are that your boss will give in. She has succeeded in
delaying the meeting two weeks, and you have succeeded in setting a
firm date for a meeting. Both of you have ''won,'' a crucial point for
successful negotiation.

The key to a successful career objective interview lies in the
preparation. Because your boss's time is limited, you must make
sure that you achieve your goals for the meeting within the time
frame. If you expect to ''wing it,'' chances are that you will never get
off the ground.

What goes into effective preparation? Focus, facts, and fit. That
is, you must determine your focus, gather the relevant facts, and see
the total organization picture and where you want to fit in it.

Focus will allow you to accomplish what you set out to accomplish within a limited time period. But remember, it's up to you
to determine that focus. In other words, know in advance what you
want the meeting to accomplish and be able to express it clearly. Pin
it down. This usually involves being able to ask for something, a task
many secretaries find difficult.

Do you want simply to state your career objectives? If this is
your first career discussion with your boss, you may simply want to
let her know where you are headed and ask for help. Do you want to
change your job title, say from secretary to assistant personnel
manager? Do you want to know how you can improve your job performance in order to move ahead in your career?

Boil down your goals for the meeting to a simple and clear core
statement. This statement is for you alone. You might, for example,
declare, ''I want to tell my boss (the sales manager) that I have
decided to pursue a career in sales,'' or ''I want to get her feedback
and support.''

Choose two or three major points that will best help achieve the
goals for the meeting. Do not plan to make every conceivable point
in support of your career objectives. The aim is to persuade your
boss, not overwhelm her.

Prepare core statements. Know what you want to say, but don't memorize. Memorized statements sound stale. Better to express your points in a variety of ways—all making the same point. For example, "I want to apply for the position of sales assistant. Sally is moving from that spot to salesperson, so her job is open. This position will get me on the career track to sales, which is the field I want to be in."

Prepare one or two questions covering the information you most need to know. Don't underestimate the time necessary to prepare these questions: to know what you don't know requires careful thought.

Asking the right questions is a very important skill at any level of an organization—particularly higher up. Since managers and executives cannot know everything, they must be aware of what they don't know—and be ready to ask the questions that will elicit the necessary information. To display this skill at the secretarial level boosts your standing as a savvy and effective employee capable of more responsibility and authority.

Have the relevant facts in your head or at hand. Here again, focus is important. The relevant facts may pertain to you and your career, to the organization, or to your boss. For example, by now you know the full range of your skills and those that are most transferable to your career objectives. Read and reread your skills inventory, and be able to give facts, such as:

* Amount of time per week that you spend on the most important skills
* Projects in which you can pinpoint your contribution
* Additional skills or training that you have acquired

Not only must you organize your thoughts about yourself (your skills, objectives, value to the organization, training needs, etc.), you must also have a clear picture of the organization's structure—both formal and informal—and some sense of where it is headed. The purpose: to identify career growth areas within it. Sarah C. Martin, who began as a secretary at City of Hope Hospital and is now associate administrator there, speaks of this step as "mental imaging of the facility as a whole"—seeing how all the parts fit together.

The ability to see the total organizational picture as well as its small components is one of the first stepping stones to career growth within an organization. Pay special attention to problem areas at your organization—the bottlenecks that stop the smooth flow of operations. If you can suggest a way you can assume additional responsibilities—perhaps even with a new job title—to eliminate a bottleneck, chances are your boss will be more receptive to your proposals. For one thing, you will have demonstrated your ability to identify substantive, not routine, problems and to suggest solutions; for another, you will stand out as an employee who has the organization's best interests at heart.

You, not your boss, are the one to "conduct" the career objective interview. Whether the interview stands on its own or is part of the performance appraisal interview (which the boss conducts), it's up to you to take charge of the discussion relating to your career objectives. That's not to say you do all of the talking. But you do determine the broad outlines of the discussion.

If you have prepared carefully for the interview, the discussion itself will go easily. Knowing in advance what you want to say will allow you to enjoy saying it and to really hear what the other person is saying. The career objective interview will be more productive the more it is handled as a two-way conversation.

There are certain messages you need to get across during the interview.

Your image as a serious career professional. Image-enhancing techniques detailed in chapters 3 and 4 apply here. The point, however, is not to act differently on the interview but to project the image of a serious career professional every day on the job, including the day of the interview.

Ambition. Ambition is not a dirty word for secretaries. But that may be a secret. Too often they have not dared to be ambitious—whether for fear of looking ridiculous, of "betraying" their bosses, or simply of failing. A sense of "what's the use?" kills ambition. But secretaries can get ahead—if they take their ambition out of the closet.

But there's a danger: how to convey your ambition without making your boss think you are after her job. This is a tricky problem. Your best bet is to show that your career growth will reflect well on your boss—that she or he is getting the fullest potential out of one of the organization's most important resources, the human resource. With some bosses it's possible, even important, to be quite bold and say, "What I really want is your job, and when you move up, I want to be ready." Of course, if your boss isn't moving up, you can't say this. In that case it's better to concentrate on the benefit to the company that would come from developing your career. You might also try to get transferred to a more dynamic boss!

Time frame. A time frame is not a threat; it is a planning device that takes into account the fact that time is limited. The time frame will commit you to change and send a signal to your organization that you are not willing to stay indefinitely if your career needs are not met. Be sure your time frame offers a range, however, not a specific date. Your organization cannot know exactly when an opening will occur. But it can keep you in mind for the next appropriate opening or can begin looking around for a suitable niche if you say that you will stay for another six months or a year.

The time frame must be realistic. If your career advancement depends on completion of a year-long course, don't say you will leave if you are not promoted within six months.

Finally, don't be afraid that time frames will alienate your boss. Any successful enterprise runs on schedules: secretaries too often overlook the fact that their career falls within a time frame, too. One way to lessen the perceived threat to your boss is to state that you will not leave her in the lurch when the organization comes up with something new; moreover, you will be available to help train your successor.

Conducting the Interview

How to get across the messages that you are a serious career professional, that you are ambitious, that you have a career time frame? There are several steps to take and much information to convey. You may not be able to cover everything in the initial interview, at least not to your full satisfaction, but don't despair: you can request follow-up interviews. Several techniques, however, can help you communicate the messages most effectively.

State Your Career Objective. Yes, once again. You've made your career decision. Now go with it! Your main task at this point is to express commitment to your decision and to get feedback from people who can help you implement it.

The advice you seek is how to reach your career objectives. Do not ask whether your boss feels the objective is realistic. This type of opener is reassuring to your boss—and self-destructive to you. You will simply be giving her the opportunity to define your career objective. In all too many cases, your boss won't want to lose a good secretary. The upshot: she will help by keeping you in your place—a no-growth position.

Use a Prepared Core Statement. A core statement is the most effective way to communicate a career objective. Do not get caught in rambling, hesitant, apologetic sentences. Get to the point immediately, and then get feedback from your boss.

Link Skills to Career Objectives. Show that your skills are transferable to your career objective. Think of yourself as a lawyer arguing a case for a client. To win the case, the lawyer must present convincing evidence to support the arguments. Your skills inventory will supply you with that evidence.

Outline Your Career Action Plan. Lay out its broad lines. These are the steps that will move you closer to your career objective. Be specific. It is easier for your boss to say yes to requests for concrete action.

• Ask for specific duties that will move you closer to your career objective. These may be brand new duties or expansions of ones you already do.

• Request the transfer of authority to cover your increased responsibilities. As you gain experience in expanded areas—say, drafting correspondence—ask for full authority to handle that task, or portions of it, on your own. Ultimate responsibility for that task would now rest with you. The point is to help your boss help you advance in your career. Both of you will win if you free your boss for tasks that require the experience and training that she has and you don't—yet.

• Ask if the organization can provide needed training and education either on the job or off. If the training and education are available only on the outside, see if the organization will foot the bill.

Invite Feedback. Solicit your boss's ideas on how to work toward your career objective. That feedback may be an evaluation of your action plan, suggestions on how to proceed and/or appraisal of your current job performance.

You need both positive and negative feedback. Many managers and supervisors, however, have trouble giving negative feedback. It's up to you to *encourage* your boss to give this information. If you are doing something wrong, or can be doing it better, find out now.

How can you encourage this information? Verbal and nonverbal cues are your best bet. They will signal that you will not fall apart when you hear criticism, you are not addicted to praise, you will not become defensive, and you will not counterattack.

Use clarifying questions and statements to get specific advice. For example, if your boss doesn't think you're assertive enough to handle an assignment, you can find this out only by saying, "I'd like to hear more about your thoughts on that" or "I need to know that type of information. Please tell me more."

The idea is to let your boss know that you want to hear more, that you appreciate the feedback. If you need even more specific information, follow up with more targeted questions. Ask, for example, "In what situations am I not assertive enough?" or "How can I be more assertive in that situation?"

Let's take another example. Suppose your boss tells you, you need more time to move ahead, that you're not ready to be an assistant buyer. Appropriate questions from you might be, "Where do you think my experience is limited?" or "What area should I concentrate on first?" or "How can I speed up this process?" or "When do you feel I would be ready?"

Asking open-ended questions can provide you with the information you need. Be specific in your questions and persist in trying to get specific answers. Vague answers reflecting vague value judgments will not be useful.

Seek Your Boss's Support. This is one of the main purposes of the career objective interview. Your boss's cooperation is obviously vital if you seek an extension of responsibility and authority within the department. Equally important is your boss's recommendation if you want to transfer to another career track within the organization. Remember, you are looking for an ally!

Two factors are important in evaluating a career objective interview: independent judgment and persistence. You must exercise both if you want this to be a useful step in building your career.

First, you have the right to evaluate your boss's response. Careful thought went into your career decision. Careful thought is required now if your boss tries to discourage you from your career-advancement action plan. Be sure to pinpoint your boss's objections; then judge for yourself whether they are justified. If they are justified, seek your boss's advice on how to modify your action plan.

However, if you decide your boss's response is not justified, nor are her suggestions helpful, reiterate your determination to work toward your career objectives. Persistence is vital. Again, your core statement is your strongest tool in driving home your point. Repeat it in response to your boss's objections, and repeat it once again. Saying it one more time might do the trick. Your core statement is the best defense against manipulative attempts by a boss to keep you "in your place".

If your boss resists your career advancement plans and fails to offer positive alternative suggestions, it is time to look elsewhere—to the personnel department and to another boss.

WORKING WITH PERSONNEL

Beverly had been secretary to the merchandise manager at a major department store in Pittsburgh for one and a half years. "My boss gave me nothing but excellent reviews," she recounts now. "He kept telling me how smart I was. In fact, he used to say, 'you remind me of a young Bonnie Green'." Bonnie Green was the store's top buyer.

Beverly smiles sardonically, recalling the incident from ten years earlier. "So I thought: if I'm so good, if I'm as smart as Bonnie Green, why shouldn't I be a buyer instead of a secretary?"

She arranged a meeting with her boss and asked to be made an assistant buyer. He looked stunned.

"No way!" he responded.

"Now it was my turn to be stunned," Beverly continues. " 'Why not?' I asked."

"You're my secretary," he said. "I didn't mean you could be a buyer."

Beverly went home very angry. She decided to go to the personnel office.

The personnel director pulled out Beverly's performance reviews. They were superb. The director called the boss, who conceded that Beverly was qualified to be an assistant buyer. There were no openings at the time, but the personnel director said Beverly would be considered for the next one.

Beverly followed up: she went to the personnel director several times to remind her she wanted to be an assistant buyer. In a fairly short time an assistant buyer's spot opened up in her boss's division. She got the job.

The importance and effectiveness of the personnel department varies from company to company. But if your boss resists your career advancement proposals, an interview with someone in personnel is a logical next step.

Attitude and persistence are the key factors in effectively using the personnel department for career advancement. Beverly had turned to her personnel department as a way to circumvent what she considered her boss's ureasonable attitude to her career plans. She adopted a positive approach toward her personnel director, and it worked.

A positive attitude toward your personnel department may find you the ally you need—someone in the department to steer you to the right job openings. It is personnel's duty, after all, to match employees with suitable advancement possibilities within the organization. If you show distrust or a lack of confidence in their willingness or ability to help, no one there will be willing to go to bat for you.

One visit alone to the personnel department is unlikely to work. You are not the only employee in the organization, and they must be concerned with all the employees. Follow-through, therefore, is crucial. Beverly paid several visits to her personnel director before the assistant buyer's spot opened. Those in the personnel department tend to admire the persistence of someone who presses forward with career advancement goals. That persistence indicates commit-ment to career objectives.

Nowhere is persistence more important than in getting the most from a job-posting system. In job-posting, an organization an-nounces its job openings, usually for a limited period of time, and allows employees to apply, or bid, for that job. A well-organized job-posting system offers an excellent chance for systematic career growth within an organization. Employees obviously gain enormous benefit from such a system. But to make it work for you, persistent follow-through is a must.

Follow-through means finding out why a job bid was rejected. If the personnel director calls to say you didn't get the job, find out why. A statement such as, "Someone with more experience got the job" is not enough. Request a face-to-face interview to get the feed-back that may make your next job bid successful.

The types of questions to ask after a job bid is turned down are, "What was the background of the person who got the job? Where did I fall short in experience? Where did I fall short in education? How can I come across better?" Make it clear that you appreciate this feedback. Again, you are seeking an ally in the department.

Above all, don't let a rejection discourage you from applying for other jobs related to your career objectives. Keep going on inter-views until you find a match. However, if you are rejected often, you may have a bad image in that company. Seek out the truth and try to straighten out the problem. If your job bids still meet with rejection, think about switching companies.

The career objective interview offers the best opportunity to enlist your boss's assistance in finding or creating the right position within the organization.

In this interview, you define the objective and your boss assists you in achieving it. It's important to keep these roles in mind, for they are a reverse of the usual boss–secretary relationship. Per-sistence is essential, because without it you risk slipping back into the traditional pattern in which the boss defines and you assist.

If your boss is not cooperative or helpful, try the personnel department. You may eventually find that a suitable position simply does not exist at your organization. Then it's time to move on.

Chapter Thirteen

Interviewing Your Prospective Boss

"No boss would put up with that type of questioning!"
"I can't do that. That's the surest way not to get the job."
"Impossible! What would he think?"
"But, I'd offend him. And then where would I be?"
"What if I wanted the job? I sure wouldn't get it."
"No way!"

The participants in the seminar were shocked and hostile. Hostile to Jodie for even daring to make a ridiculous suggestion.

The suggestion? That the secretary has the right to interview a prospective boss. That it isn't just up to the boss to choose her, it is also up to her to choose the boss. And that she could ask questions that could help her arrive at an intelligent decision about whether this was the right boss and the right career-positioning job.

The initial job interview sets the tone for the secretary–boss relationship. If the secretary is passive in the interview, if she asks only routine questions (e.g., about fringe benefits) while the boss asks the probing ones (e.g., job attitudes), and if she shows no concern for her career future, chances are that on the job she will be passive, short-sighted, and fearful about moving ahead.

What we're saying is very simple: if you want to take control of your career, you must assume a take-charge attitude from the very beginning—from the initial interview. You must enter an employment relationship with your eyes open and your aims clear. And the best eye-opener is the interview.

What about the fears expressed in the opening comments of this chapter? Will you offend a potential boss by asking career-positioning questions on a job interview? Does asking these questions endanger your chance of getting the job?

The answer is not simple. Asking career-positioning questions may offend a prospective boss, but it may impress the boss who will help you with your career. If a boss indicates that he wants a compliant secretary who follows orders blindly, or who will stay in a no-growth job for ten years, do you want that job? The choice is not up to the boss. It is *your* career.

The right boss is very important for career advancement. Finding such a boss is your responsibility.

The right attitudes are the key to finding the right prospective boss. Bring to the interview the self-knowledge, the self-acceptance, and the assertive self-definition that project the image of a competent professional.

Your secretarial skills can get you a secretarial job very easily today. But your aim is not to get just any job but to get a job that will allow you to develop the skills necessary for your long-term career objectives.

"Sounds good," you may be thinking, "but I have to eat. I can't afford to be independent. I need a job!"

Which brings us to an important tip about how *not* to approach the career-positioning job interview: not in desperation! Desperation stands in the way of your adopting the assertive, independent approach necessary to land the career-positioning job.

We don't mean to imply that finding the right job is easy. All we're saying is that it is possible if you make the right moves. And you are less likely to make the right moves if you are desperate for *any* job.

We're also saying that today a secretary needn't be desperate for any job. Secretaries are in demand. While you search for that career-positioning job, you can work at a standard secretarial job—it brings in a weekly salary. Or, you may choose to work as an office temporary. Myrna helped to finance her own career-positioning with temp work. First she used it to help pay for graduate school and then to bring home some money while taking a stab at free-lance writing. Temp work can tide you over during your search for the career positioning job. But remember: for you, the no-growth secretarial job and temp work are only means to an end, not ends in themselves.

The prospective boss has set interview goals before an applicant even shows up: to fill the opening with the most qualified candidate. You must likewise set your goals for the interview. These are:

• To find the career-building job. Getting such a job is the only way to take control of your career. The career-positioning job translates into your short-term career goal.

• To get information—about the job, the company, and the boss. Getting information about the job and the company are obviously essential: What does the job consist of? What are the duties? What skills will be used? What is the growth potential on the job and within the company? What is the company's mission, objectives, attitude toward employees?

Equally essential, however, and somehow often overlooked, is the necessity to get information about the boss. After all, the purpose of the interview from the boss's point of view is to get as much information as possible about you. How else can someone determine if you're the right one for the job? Similarly, you need information about the boss. What is his or her attitude toward a secretary? How does he envision the job? Does he appear rigid? Humorless? Does he want a secretary to get his coffee? Can you learn from this person? Is he dynamic? What is his philosophy of work? Does he show signs of being a workaholic? Does he expect his employees to be workaholics? You must:

• Weed out the wrong type of boss. Once you have the information, weigh it. Be discriminating. Is this person really the boss you want to work for? Will he encourage your career advancement? Is he open to expanding the job along lines that lead to your career objective?

• Determine if the boss's secretarial needs match your career needs. Can you learn new skills while fully using those you have? Do you and the boss see the job in the same way? Do you have a match?

BEFORE THE INTERVIEW

Preparation for a job interview with a prospective boss is even more important than for the interview with a current boss. This job interview may be the only opportunity for you to evaluate each other. Only careful preparation will ensure that you give the information you want to give and obtain the information you need.

Much of the preparation for the interview with a prospective boss is the same as for one with a current boss, which we discussed in the previous chapter. In the two situations, you determine your focus, gather the relevant facts, and see where you fit within the total organizational picture. Rather than repeat the guidelines given in chapter 12, we'll focus here on what is different about preparing for the interview with a prospective boss.

An obvious and necessary technique is to prepare several major questions to ask the boss. You must find out at the beginning how much room there is for initiative on this job, how much responsibility is assigned, how much authority is delegated. Ask for examples of specific problems you might face immediately, perhaps because the predecessor had failed to do the tasks properly or because the boss wants to expand the role of the newly hired person.

A less obvious, though no less necessary technique is to prepare several questions that you want your prospective boss to ask you. Preparing these questions will help you formulate what key information you think your boss needs to appreciate what you can offer the organization. If the boss does ask these questions, chances are the two of you are thinking along the same lines, that is, the boss is looking for an able, take-charge, promotable person. If your boss does not ask the questions, work their answers into the interview on your own.

These questions, and the answers, should focus on your job skills—with particular attention given to your ability to solve problems, make decisions, deal with people, and organize. In addition, they should explore your short-term and long-term career objectives (how you envision the job for which you are applying and how you see it within your overall career goals). These questions should also identify your major achievements on and off the job.

Preparing for an interview with a prospective boss in your current organization offers inside sources of information. Ask other people what it's like working for the prospective boss. Ask other secretaries in that department. Use the secretarial grapevine, but don't rely on casual, vague comments. And don't rely simply on the boss's reputation. Find out the particulars behind that reputation. Do different people see this boss differently? What are the points of difference? Get the specifics.

Perhaps most important of all, find out where the prospective boss's previous secretaries have moved to. Have they been promoted? With the boss's support? Have they moved outside the organization because this person wanted *just* a secretary?

Of course you should keep in mind that a prospective boss within your company has additional sources of information about you, too. He can talk with your current or former bosses. He can look at your personnel file. He, too, may have access to the secretarial grapevine. Be aware of the picture that the prospective boss will likely have of you before you even step into the office.

Gathering worthwhile information on an outside company is nearly impossible. If you are lucky, however, you may know someone, or someone who knows someone, within the new organization. Turn to this source for the type of inside information we recommended above.

Information about your fit within the prospective organization will be very scanty—and probably will come from employees already working there. The "mental imaging of the facility as a whole," to repeat Sarah Martin's phrase, comes only with knowledge gained working within the organization.

Analyzing past interviews can provide valuable tips for success on future ones. Can you remember the sinking feeling you got when you left an interview—either that you said something you shouldn't have or that you didn't say something you should have? Recall now your interview post mortems and learn from them. It's the only way not to repeat past mistakes.

Pay particular attention to the interviews that resulted in a job. How did those interviews reflect characteristics of the boss? Did the boss send off clues—verbal and nonverbal—that you ignored, much to your later dismay on the job? For example, did your boss take outside telephone calls during the interview and then resume talking with you without apology or explanation? Did this casual disregard foreshadow his treatment of you once you became his secretary? Now is the time to identify those clues and be prepared to spot them in upcoming interviews.

DURING THE INTERVIEW

If we were to choose one piece of advice to offer the secretary on an interview with a prospective boss, it is: BE ALERT!

Sound easy? It's not. You must not only say what you want to say and obtain the information you need, you must also be alert to nonverbal clues. Reading these is tricky—mainly it boils down to your intuition. Read between the lines. Beware of empty phrases. For example, the boss might speak in vague terms of "potential for growth." Do you know what she has in mind? Does she? Find out! Don't be conned by vague promises and buzzwords.

An interview with a prospective boss will follow a format. Although the specifics may vary from interview to interview, certain general points are essential.

Your first task is to get a job description from the prospective boss. What does the job involve? What type of secretary is he looking for?

Beware if the boss starts off with the question, "Tell me about yourself." This is a difficult question to answer. Where on earth do you begin? You begin by deflecting the question back to the boss.

You may respond with a statement that poses its own question: "I'd appreciate it if you would tell me first about the job and what

DO'S AND DON'TS FOR ASKING QUESTIONS

DON'T use an abrasive style.
  DO use an assertive style.
DON'T be apologetic asking the questions.
  DO be confident.
DON'T bark questions at the interviewer.
  DO use a pleasant tone of voice.
DON'T prepare questions the interviewer won't know the answers to.
  DO stay away from "show-off" questions.
DON'T ask too many questions—rapid-fire volley will be more an interrogation than an interview.
  DO ask the few questions of greatest importance to you.
DON'T ask questions simply to make a good impression.
  DO ask questions that make the boss feel you are really interested in the company and the job.

your priorities are." "It'll help me organize my answer if you first tell me what type of duties I'd be helping you with." "I'd like to relate my experience to the job, so perhaps you could help by telling me first what the job involves."

This response is bold but not unreasonable. If the boss answers your question without fuss and then tries to find out your qualifications for the job, you're talking with someone who would respect your independence and your desire for a fulfilling job with growth potential. If, on the other hand, the response is: "You're here to type, take steno, and be a secretary. Don't you know what that means?" watch out! This boss is unlikely to value your desire to get ahead or help you reach your career goals. Why would you want to work for such a boss?

If the response is, "What is this? I feel you're interviewing me," don't be apologetic. Simply explain your point of view: "We're interviewing each other. It's very important that I know what you want and can meet your needs."

The point to remember is that there is nothing wrong with interviewing a prospective boss. To the contrary, it demonstrates a seriousness of purpose, a commitment to career objectives. You are standing behind your image as a professional who is a secretary but not *just* a secretary. Communicate the right image from the beginning and you will find a boss who not only accepts your career goals but will actively support them.

Next comes your turn to tell why you are qualified for the job. Describe your skills and achievements. Give special emphasis to the transferable skills that can be applied to your career objectives. Give specific examples of problems you have solved on your own, decisions you have made, office or other systems you have organized, and types of people (customers, clients, other secretaries) you have worked well with. Or, perhaps you have offered suggestions that have contributed to decisions or solutions devised by your boss. These, too, are relevant. Look for your contributions in the nonroutine aspects of your job, those that go beyond your daily clerical functions.

Show how your skills and achievements have benefited the organization, If you were involved in a profitable project, don't be shy about identifying the dollar-and-cents payoff for the company. Of course, projects in which you had a major responsibility will be of greatest interest to the prospective employer. However, it may be that your responsibility was only as a member of a team that worked on the project. This, too, would be of interest. A boss is most effective as the head of a team of intelligent, responsible, discerning employees.

Describe only your strengths. When you give information about yourself, don't go off on tangents. Shortcomings are tangents that are irrelevant to your qualifications for the job. You want to persuade the prospective boss of what you can do, not what you cannot do. Let the boss know how you can help.

Share your career objectives and your schedule for achieving them with the prospective boss. Let him or her know where you want your career to head. The two of you are at the shopping stage, and each of you should know what the other has in mind for the future. But be reasonable. The prospective boss is now looking for a secretary, not a sales manager or a personnel director or a buyer. The boss needs to know that you are committed to working as a secretary—and working hard at that—for a period of time while you develop the skills and gain the experience that will lead to the next step in your career. Nothing will turn an interviewer off faster than the thought that three months from now this very competent secretary will leave for greener pastures.

In other words, being a secretary, and remaining a secretary for a period of time, is part of your career action plan. It is important to assure the prospective boss of your commitment, not just to your long-term career objective but also to your short-term goal—to be a good secretary.

Should you commit yourself to stay for a specific period of time? We would advise against it. Careers are fluid. It's hard to tell how long it will be before you are ready to move on. Also, if you plan to find the next career-positioning job at the same organization, you may have to wait until there is a suitable opening.

But just because you do not specify an exact date by which you want to move on, you certainly can communicate a general time frame for this stage of your career. You can, for example, say that you would plan to remain in the secretarial spot for one or two years while you learn as much as possible for the next steps in your career plan. You can also assure the person of your sense of responsibility in the job: you will not leave someone in the lurch at the first sign of another position. And finally, you may tell the interviewer that if the secretarial position expands to suit your need for growth and challenge, you could easily remain in it for more than one or two years.

What you are doing at this stage of the interview is persuading the boss of your sense of responsibility regarding the available position, your seriousness about doing a good job, and your determination to develop a career to fit your objectives.

Any reasonable boss will recognize that there must always be a tradeoff between quality and time. An A1 secretary is going to move on and up—all really good employees do. If the boss doesn't want to recognize this, he's going to end up with mediocre help.

The boss will want to get a clearer picture of your background. For example, you may be asked why you left your last job, or why you want to leave your current one. Don't fall into the trap of bad-mouthing a past or current employer. Always emphasize the positive—for example, you learned as much as possible at the job and now want to move on.

Understand what's important in your responses. There really is no right or wrong answer. The other person's aim is to get the flavor of you as a person and as a employee. How do you come across? Are you the type of person she or he wants to work with?

Equally important, is this the type of person you want to work with? Two types of questions will help you find out more specifics about the job—and the boss. One set will define the exact nature of the job; the other will give you a clearer picture of the potential for career development. Some examples of each type follow.

Job-Clarifying Questions
    What are the major tasks of this job?
    What are your priorities for the secretary's responsibilities?
    In what types of situations does your secretary solve problems, make decisions, deal with people?

Once I complete the routine aspects of the job, how much opportunity would I have to handle the nonroutine matters?
How can I use my organizational abilities on this job?
Do you travel a lot on the job? Can you estimate the percentage of time you would be out of the office?
When you are out, what are my responsibilities?

Career-Positioning Questions
Where are your past secretaries now? What positions do they hold?
Have any previous secretaries moved up to better jobs in or outside the company?
Can a secretary become a _____ in this company? (Buyer, for example)
Can I develop skills as your secretary that would help me move into the [buyer's] career track?
What are the promotion opportunities for a secretary within this company?
Is there opportunity on this job to move to an entry-level [buyer's] position?
Does this company have job-posting?
Are *all* available openings posted? Which are not?
Is anyone who is qualified interviewed for the job?
Is feedback given?
Does the company limit the number or type of job bids an employee can make. If so, what are these limits?
Note: A job-posting system in which companies announce job openings for which employees may apply seems to promise upward mobility. However, systems vary from company to company, and you must find out whether there is anything behind the promise. The crucial point is to learn whether secretaries can bid for job openings outside the secretarial field.

Other job-qualifying and career-positioning subjects to clarify include:

education and training possibilities
performance appraisal systems
fringe benefits
salary review system

Secretaries generally feel most comfortable asking about these subjects, particularly the last two, because they seem ''safer.'' We don't deny their importance, but we do want you to be aware that other issues have greater significance for your career development—and those are the ones to concentrate on. Moreover, an overconcern with fringe benefits seems almost beside the point for an employee determined to move on and up. Don't give the wrong message to prospective employers.

Clarify the prospective boss's statements—then clarify some more. Make sure you understand what this person does and does not say.

For example, suppose the prospective boss said, "It's tough but not impossible" when you asked whether a secretary could become a buyer in that company. What does this response mean? You'll need to ask clarifying questions, such as: Have any of your secretaries been able to make the switch? When you say, "not impossible," do you have a particular person in mind? When you say "tough," do you mean that some secretaries have tried to make the move and failed? What seems to hold secretaries back from promotion within the company?

An example of a promising response? "If you're a good secretary, I'll teach you a lot about buying. I need someone to help me."

"I don't think it's very likely" may be considered discouraging, although it may just be realistic. It's worth exploring further, however.

Suppose the initial response was very negative: "I'm not looking for a secretary to be an assistant. This is just a secretary's job." Our advice? Look elsewhere.

At this point, both of you may suspect you're not a good match. If you know for sure, thank him for the interview and say the job isn't what you're looking for at this stage in your career. Then leave.

However, you may want to make sure that you have the right picture: "Then do I understand correctly that this is a straight typing and filing job without much chance for career growth?" If the answer is yes, it's time to conclude the interview.

Suppose the company is right but the boss or job is wrong. In that case, try to find out what other opportunities are available:

"This job doesn't seem right for me at this point in my career. However, I'm very interested in the company. Are there other openings more suited to my background and my career objectives?"

It's a long shot, but the interviewer may provide other leads. You have nothing to lose by asking.

Alternatively, at this point you both may suspect a match: You're right for the job and the job is right for you. The next step? The boss will try to "sell" you the job by making an offer you can't refuse. It generally is at this stage that the prospective boss will bring up fringe benefits and salary.

Now is the time to negotiate for a better salary. Remember, at this point the boss is the seller and you are the buyer. If the salary is too low, say so. For example:

"I'm very interested in the job, but I'm looking for a higher starting salary. I want to start off at _____ dollars."

Some negotiating may now take place. You'll handle yourself better if you have read one or two of the recent popular books on the subject. The principles of negotiating, by the way, are useful for many aspects of our lives, not just for salary discussions.

The conclusion to a job interview varies from company to company. Sometimes the boss will make the job offer; sometimes you will be sent to the personnel department.

When an offer is made, don't respond immediately. Always take at least twenty-four hours to analyze the interview—the boss's statements, the nonverbal messages you received about the boss and the company, the formal job description, and the growth potential for your career. Don't be intimidated into giving an immediate answer. A gracious but delaying comment can be:

"The job sounds terrific, but I need a day to think about it. I'll call Monday with my response."

If you like what you have heard and seen, why do you need the extra time to think about it? Because your career is important, and it's important to sort out all your impressions before committing yourself to a career-positioning job. A delay does not indicate indecisiveness but rather deliberateness. A boss who presses for an immediate answer is unlikely to respect your independence on the job.

Sometimes, however, there is no firm job offer. The interview may conclude with, "We'll get back to you." This may not be an encouraging sign, especially if it's not followed up with specifics about when and how. Try to get information so you are not left dangling indefinitely. If you are interested in the job, make that clear: "The job does sound as if it's what I'm looking for. I hope you'll consider me for it. When can I expect to hear from you?" Then thank the person for the interview, shake hands, and leave.

READING THE PROSPECTIVE BOSS RIGHT

Finding the right boss is one of your primary goals on the interview. It is a big challenge, for you will need to weigh many factors and sift through many messages before making a decision.

There are clues to look for in the boss's comments and behavior to help you decide if you're right for each other, if the right chemistry and flow exists between you. But remember, clues must be evaluated. Your independent judgment has the final say.

The right prospective boss listens to you attentively. You know he is listening by his steady eye-contact, facial expression, responses, and the "free information" he gives about the job and about himself.

Listening requires undivided attention. Does he answer phone calls or fiddle with papers while you're talking? If he's interrupted, does he offer reasons for the distraction? Does he look bored? Is he leaning toward you, a sign he is listening?

The right prospective boss shows interest in your achievements. He asks questions about them, and his face registers his approval. If you get the feeling that he couldn't care less about your accomplishments, then you are interviewing a boss whose prospects for you are not promising.

The right propsective boss says the job holds career growth potential and ties in with your career objectives. But watch out for the con. Try to get him to talk in specifics. Also watch out for his reaction to your open avowal of ambition. The right boss does not appear threatened nor look shocked or angry when you state your career objectives.

The right prospective boss describes what he or the job can teach you in preparation for your next career step. He encourages your desire to learn new skills and to further develop existing ones.

The right prospective boss not only says what he requires of you but responds positively to what you require of him. He does not send off signals that you are "his property", that you must sacrifice your goals, needs, and ambitions on the altar of his career, that you owe your primary loyalty to him.

The prospective boss gives off signs that he is on your side, that he will go to bat for you in your effort to develop a job that meets your career objectives. This boss will not view the secretarial position as a dead-end. Personal and professional growth are possible for secretaries—and the boss is an important factor in this growth. The right boss is worth a long and careful search.

But suppose you didn't read the prospective boss right. What if the boss with whom you established such good rapport during the interview fails to deliver once you accept the job—and you find yourself, once again, *just* a secretary?

Then it's time to start looking for a better boss and a better job. A losing career move need not be forever. And when you begin your search once again you can benefit from the lessons learned during the previous round of interviews.

A secretary aware of her skills and potential, committed to her objectives, and determined to move ahead will find the right boss and the right job. But it may take more time. Just keep at it.

Chapter Fourteen

Moving Ahead with Office Automation

Office automation is the application of new electronic technologies to such simple office tasks as typing and filing as well as to more complex functions such as decision-making and problem-solving. Most offices will move to automation in the near future because the declining cost of the technology will make the equipment more and more affordable. Office automation will offer you new opportunities for job enrichment, work satisfaction, and career advancement.

Six years ago, Barbara was a secretary at a company that had just gotten it's first word processor. Today she is manager of the Office Automation Department and Projects Group at a major New York bank.

How did she make the transition? By taking the initiative. Her secretarial job did not require her to use the new word processor, but seeing the opportunity for a career change, she taught herself to operate it. A whole new world opened.

Using her hands-on experience in word processing and her excellent communication skills, she landed a job selling automated office equipment. Presto! She had gotten rid of the secretarial title. After more experience in the field, she got a job as a market support representative, advising customers on effective use of the equipment.

She was on her way to her long-term career objective: a management position in office automation. Within five years she had achieved her objective.

Elly took the initiative, too. An executive secretary for fifteen years, Elly heard, via the grapevine, that her company was thinking about installing word processors in one department. A friend in another company that had automated swore by the word-processor—it allowed her to get her typing out faster and freed up time for more interesting projects.

Elly saw an opportunity and she grabbed it. She asked her boss to send her to an intensive one week word-processing course offered to companies that purchased the equipment. Her boss agreed: Elly was just the one to bring back the information about how to operate the equipment and how to use it to turn out the department's work. A top-flight secretary, Elly was in her forties, with two years of college behind her and an aptitude for math and science.

Elly was excited. She was also scared. "At my age," she told us, "learning something completely new was quite a challenge." But she plunged into the task enthusiastically and returned from the course determined to learn as much as she could about office automation: she stayed late after work and played with the word processor, figuring out new applications. "The more you use the equipment," she says, "the more applications you discover."

In less than six months, Elly was a dynamo in word processing and persuaded her boss that the whole department should be tied into the system. There are now four word processors in the department and Elly has helped other secretaries use the equipment after they returned from their one week course. She is the acknowledged expert in word-processing applications within her company. More and more departments are acquiring word processors, and Elly's expertise becomes more valuable by the day. And not just to the company.

Doors outside are opening as well. The vendor of the word-processing equipment purchased by Elly's firm has offered her a job as a market support representative. "They call *me* for advice if one of their customers has a problem," Elly said recently. "I know more about the equipment than their sales rep because I use it."

Both Elly and Barbara grabbed the initiative in using office automation to enhance their careers. But both found their opportunities in different areas. Elly became an expert on the technical side of automation, on how the equipment can be used to do the department's work. Barbara used the equipment to perform administrative functions and worked her way into management. We say more about the division between the technical side and the administrative side later in this chapter. For now, keep Elly's and Barbara's cases in mind. They both point to success.

The introduction of office automation is an "event," says Mitch Goldstein, an office automation expert. It can transform the secretary's job, whether she chooses to remain a secretary or to move into other areas.

Consider how the word processor transformed Georgie's job. Georgie is the secretary to the president of a small New York company. The word processor got rid of a lot of her boring, routine work. "Instead of typing the same letter fifty or a hundred times," she reports, "I now type it into the word processor once and then simply type the names and addresses of the people who are to get it. The machine does the rest. That frees me to help my boss and the vice president of finances with other things. For example, I have the time to help prepare payroll, to keep track of insurance claim forms, to coordinate the installation of phones. That's really what I like to do! I *like* to organize and coordinate. And I'm good at it."

But to really use the "event," to transform it into your personal Independence Day, you must apply many of our other tips for career advancement. In other words, don't think of office automation as a brand new phenomenon requiring brand new ways of thinking and acting. Rather, think of it as a brand new opportunity for applying many of the commonsense rules for self-assertion and career advancement. Use office automation as the wedge with which to open up a rewarding, challenging career.

Office automation will not automatically sweep you into a great new job. In fact, unless you plan how to take advantage of the new technologies, office automation may make your job more fragmented and more routine. In other words, you can use the time freed up by office automation to take on more challenging responsibilities, or you may end up using it to type more memos and more correspondence. You can have a say in the result.

For those of you who have not yet chosen your career objectives or settled on a career action plan, office automation offers the exciting opportunity of a new frontier. Explore the field. See whether you like it. See how your talents and skills can be put to use. See where you want to fit in.

A WINNING CAREER STRATEGY

But how to get started? How to devise the winning career strategy that uses the event of office automation? Although we focus on strategies to use within a company that is "going automated", most of the strategies also apply for secretaries working in companies already partially or fully automated. The key for both groups is to seize the initiative—target objectives, acquire skills, and get a job reclassification.

There are six steps that will help you make the most of the new technology:

- Find out how the organization will change.
- Weigh the information—and plan your moves.
- Expand the job.
- Get experience.
- Fight for a job reclassification.
- Move ahead.

Find Out How the Organization Will Change. Office automation is not only an event, it is a *big* event. This is true for your organization, and it is true for your career. As with all big events, there will be a lot of talk about it. Information will float around the organization, some of which will be true and some of which will be false. Your initial task is to gather as much true information as possible—what, where, when, and how changes will take place. Only then can you make plans for how to profit from the event. Your main sources of information about organizational changes could be the grapevine, consultants, your boss, and the sponsoring department.

News of automation may hit first via the grapevine, your early alert system. From experience, however, you undoubtedly know the grapevine often does not discriminate between true and false. Begin immediately to get more substantial information.

A source of substantial information may be the consultants who come into an organization to plan and implement the automation move. In the past consultants got their information only from company managers and executives, not from the people actually operating and using the equipment. As a result, equipment was imposed on the employees using it, and failure was common. Today, however, the users are more likely to be consulted and their needs considered. Experience has shown consultants that users can make the difference between the success or failure of office automation within an organization.

You are a potential user. The consultant needs your knowledge of the organization to introduce the right equipment for a successful switchover to automation. You know what work must get out, to whom, when, for what purpose, who does the work now and in what way, what standard problems are encountered, and so on. In other words, the consultant needs your information to be successful. But you also need the consultant's information to learn how office automation can be a plus in your career.

Help the consultant make the changeover a success by sharing your information. But at the same time, get as much information as possible from the consultant. Ask questions such as: What changes will occur? What will be the staffing needs? How will the automated equipment change my job? How can I personally help to make the switchover a success? How can automation help me advance in my career? What positions in the organization will offer advancement opportunities as a result of automation? How and where can I learn more about automation? What problems with automation should I be aware of? How can I cope with the problems? Will the organization restructure to accommodate automation? How?

A switchover to automation is a pivotal event for your boss as well. She may be able to fill you in on more information about the change—and, particularly, how it will affect you. Notice we said *may*. Your boss's information, at least in the early stages, may not be much better than yours. This is particularly true when automation is implemented without a formal strategic plan and without consultants. Most companies fall into this category. The result: people don't know what's going on. Your boss may be one of those mystified by this major event. This is your chance to shine. Whenever there is a void in an organization, whenever there is the need to create order out of chaos, there is the opportunity for you to pitch in and help improve the situation. Look for these voids. They are your key opportunity spots—always.

What kind of information can the boss provide at this point? She can tell you what she knows of the change. Ask her questions. Many are similar to those we suggested you ask of the consultant: What are our plans? What departments will be involved? What new equipment will be brought in? What kind of help do you need to make the change a success? Where can I fit in?

Some organizations will restructure to accommodate office automation; others won't. If your company is restructuring, find out as much about it as possible from your boss. The reason: each organization will use different equipment and will restructure differently according to its needs. Your aim is to mesh your needs with the organization's, to make the automation changeover a success and to create a challenging and rewarding career for you.

The restructuring may divide functions between the administrative and the technical. Mitch Goldstein, the office automation consultant, explains it this way: the administrative side is where the work is coming from; the technical side is where the work is done. An executive secretary or office manager would be on the administrative side; a word processor operator, supervisor, or manager would be on the technical. In some organizations the word process-

ing (only one of the technologies in office automation) would be performed in a word-processing center and the administrative work
would be performed in the general office. The secretary in the
general office would use the output of the word-processing center
rather than work there. Office automation could take the heavy typing off this secretary's hands, allowing her more time to coordinate
office functions and take on more challenging work.

In other organizations, no fundamental restructuring will occur. In these companies the secretary would continue to type, but the
word processor would allow her to do it faster. The saved time could
be channeled toward more challenging tasks.

The grapevine, consultants, and your boss were sources of information about organizational changes. Now it's time to research
office automation itself. At this stage your aim is to get a broad picture. Learn the names of the equipment and what each type
does—electronic typewriters, word processors, personal computers,
computer terminals, work stations, electronic mail systems, electronic filing systems, teleconferencing. Magazine and newspaper articles will tell you what equipment is available now and what will be
available in the future, how the equipment affects office jobs, how it
helps or hinders the secretary's job, what are the pluses and minuses
of the different types of equipment. Visits to trade shows and computer stores can also give you a better idea of the ''office of the
future''

Weigh the Information—and Plan Your Moves. By now, you
probably have a good deal of information. But do you have a good
idea of how it all adds up?

Take some time to think about what you've learned. Sort out
your impressions. Figure out where your interests lie. Do you lean
toward the technical or administrative side of office automation?
You probably already have an inkling. For example, if you like
machines and are good with equipment you might want to channel
your energies toward the technical side. If you want to take over
some of your boss's job, you will want to focus on how the equipment can be used for administrative functions. Decide where the opportunities are for you. Begin thinking of career objectives that tie in
with office automation.

Above all, don't sit back and simply wait until the higher-ups
decide what you will do with the time freed by office automation.
Chances are your organization is not yet sure how to mesh the
employees with the equipment, in jobs that will produce the best
results for the organization. Be ready to offer your ideas.

Say you have set your sights on moving into management. Your aim, then, would be to increase your administrative functions. For this, you need your boss's cooperation and support. *She* must delegate increased responsibility and authority. Your planning—in other words, strategy—becomes vital.

N. Dean Meyer, an advanced office automation specialist, offers a winning strategy: figure out what higher-level managerial work your boss wants to do more of but doesn't have time for because of her routine managerial tasks. This is your opening. Plan to show your boss how, with a computer, you can take over many of her routine duties, such as pulling together information. This would free *her* for more important functions.

By emphasizing the positive—showing how she can benefit by upgrading your functions—you can persuade your boss that she'll look good when you look good. And you can accomplish this without appearing to threaten her job. Office automation will help both of you perform more effectively.

Moving up the office automation ladder typically takes place in two stages. The first stage usually involves expansion of the secretary's responsibilities as she carries out her old tasks, begins to get office automation experience, and takes on new responsibilities with the time freed by office automation productivity. The second stage, after she has become thoroughly familiar with office automation equipment and procedures and with her new responsibilities, should find her seeking formal recognition of her new role in the company.

Expand the job. Once you decide what you want to do, don't keep your objectives to yourself. Let you boss know. Let your personnel director know.

And volunteer. Volunteer for the additional tasks and responsibilities that you just targeted in your planning. This is the best way to carve out the job you want. For example, volunteer to attend courses in word processing, or even more forward-looking, the use of personal computers. Try to get the company to pay. If it refuses, foot the bill yourself. It's an investment in your career—an investment in yourself.

The techniques employed in the performance appraisal or career objective interview offer the best approach for discussing with your boss how office automation can boost your career and increase your effectiveness on the job. But don't wait another six months until you are due for a performance appraisal! Set up an appointment with your boss as soon as possible.

Your strongest communication technique is the core statement.

Use it when discussing the expansion of your job. Where possible, try to work in examples of how your boss will benefit. Be positive about office automation and its potential for both you and your boss. And, without being blustery or threatening, be persistent in pursuing functions you want to perform or courses you want to take. It's your future, so grab it.

Get the experience. Office automation offers a brand new set of tools. The more you learn about the equipment, the more effectively you will be able to use it—and the more it will be a plus for your career. The learning process for any of the types of equipment is similar. But we will use word processors as an example.

First, get the basics under your belt. Most vendors offer a brief course of instruction along with purchase of the word processors. But understand, this course gives you only the bare essentials. It's up to you to fill in the details by reading the operator's manual and, more important, by doing.

In fact, you can pick up the basics on your own, even without an introductory course. Barbara, the bank office automation manager, taught herself to use word processors by observing others working with the equipment, by reading the manual, and by practicing on the machines.

Use the equipment. Experiment. Play with it. Playing with the equipment is an important part of the learning process. Don't just look at the keys on the terminal; find out what they do. Use them! The best way to "play" with a word processor is to set up a test document. Use the keys: delete characters, switch paragraphs, try out the other features. If you "destroy" the document by touching the wrong key, nothing important is lost—chalk it up to the learning process.

Don't worry about the complex details of the technology. As Peter F. Drucker, a leading management consultant, has pointed out, it's not necessary to know how the telephone works to be able to use it effectively.

Playing with the equipment will help you discover what it can and cannot do. Put the emphasis on "can." Understand what your boss needs done and then figure out how the automated equipment will help you do it. "The more you use the equipment," as Elly said at the beginning of this chapter, "the more applications you discover."

Look at the automated equipment as a tool to aid in performing your duties more effectively. *It* is your assistant.

Once you know the basics, learn more details about how to use the equipment. There are several ways to do this:

• Take courses. Seek out the many schools and colleges that offer courses in office automation. Select the courses which fit your needs.

• Read up on office automation. Books on practice, not theory, are the ones to look for. Books, magazines, trade journals, vendor advertisements, and the business press will supply you with more details on the various types of equipment.

• Attend trade shows. They'll show you the newest in automated office equipment. Market support representatives are generally available at these shows and are glad to answer questions. Trade shows are also a good place to make contacts which you can later follow up on when looking for a job.

• Join professional organizations. Groups of people involved in office automation will provide opportunities for learning more about the field from those in it. They also make a valuable network of contacts for jobs (see the appendix for the names of two leading organizations).

Fight for a job reclassification. Once you have gained hands-on experience with automated equipment, be ready to market that experience—and yourself. This step calls for job reclassification, and in most cases it doesn't come automatically. You must ask for it—persuasively and persistently. In other words, it's up to you to point out to your boss or your personnel director that you have acquired new experience and you want a new job title to reflect your new functions. For example, if you work in the personnel department and have assumed personnel functions, ask for a job reclassification to personnel assistant or assistant personnel manager. Work out the exact title with your boss.

Requests for job reclassification could sound something like this: ''I would like a job reclassification to word-processing supervisor. I'm not a secretary any more: I spend most of my time advising others on how to use the equipment. As supervisor, I can work with secretaries when they return from their word-processing course, and I can teach them new applications for the equipment. We need someone to coordinate the increased work flow, and I can handle it if we get someone else to take over my secretarial responsibilities. I'll be here to supervise the new secretary.'' Or you might say: ''I would like a job reclassification to public relations assistant. I now spend a good part of my day writing press releases, contacting the press, and smoothing out problems with clients. Typing and filing take up a very small portion of my day.''

If your first request for job reclassification doesn't work, try again—soon. And again. Stress your career objective and your determination to work toward it. Point out that job reclassification is a vital step in moving ahead. Keep stressing your new skills and your new experience—and your increased value to your boss and to the organization. Volunteer to train others in departments that are just starting to automate. You may be able to position yourself and reclassify your job in another department in the company. If repeated requests are rejected, ask if job reclassification will ever be possible at that company. Pin down a date. If you're not satisfied with the response, start looking for a job elsewhere.

Move ahead. After you win your new job title and gain more experience in the position, it may be time to prepare yourself to move on. Find out what higher-level jobs are within reach in your department and what skills or additional knowledge you may need to qualify for them. Target a position in line with your interests, skills, and needs.

If you can't find a higher-level position in your department, try to find a spot elsewhere in the organization. Try to get your boss's support for a move. Talk to your personnel director about opportunities in other departments. If your company can't provide a suitable higher-level position, move to a company that will. Your new job title will help. A company just beginning to automate might have just what you're looking for. In other words, you would be coming on board as an experienced user of automated equipment.

How do you get leads for jobs at such companies? Contacts are invaluable here. If you have joined an office automation professional organization, spread the word that you are looking for a job and specify your target level. Your vendor's sales representative may be another good source of job leads. The reps have inside information of companies that have just purchased equipment and seek experienced users. Be aware, however, that working through the sales rep when you are still employed at the company with which he or she deals is a delicate situation—for both of you. Getting this information requires a close business relationship. Still another good, if unconventional, source of job leads is the equipment service person, who may know of vacancies at other companies.

Office automation vendors offer some of the best career opportunities for advancement into management. The industry is still new and movement within it can be speedier than in older, more established industries.

Sales, training, and customer service positions are good take-off points for career advancement in the office automation industry. Secretaries who gain their experience in an automated office will find that many of their skills are transferable. What does a secretary bring to these jobs? Her familiarity with the equipment, her knowledge of office procedures, her organizational and coordination ability, and, above all, her communication skills.

Office automation offers the secretary a wedge with which to open up rewarding jobs. Whether on the administrative side or the technical side, there are new opportunities. But you must move now. Take advantage of the still wide open field. Users and vendors alike have a need for qualified people to facilitate the switch to office automation.

As a top-notch secretary, you are qualified to help make automation work in your company or other companies. You have "company smarts". Use them to make office automation succeed. Adopt a positive attitude.

What goes into a positive attitude toward the "office of the future"? Three things above all: flexibility, adaptability, and assertiveness.

These are the traits you will need to succeed in the automated office. The equipment is changing rapidly. If you use the equipment, you must change with it. In other words, you must face the challenge of rapid change—and go with it. Fighting the forces of change is a losing proposition.

Don't succumb to technology terror—the I-can't-do-it-and-never-will-be-able-to syndrome. It will short-circuit your effectiveness and curtail your career possibilities. With flexibility, adaptability, and assertiveness, you *can* do it. All you need is the willingness to learn—and grow.

Chapter Fifteen

Reaching Out and Taking Chances

Career development is what this book is all about; career development and self-development. It's about recognizing the value and transferability of your secretarial skills.

Adopt the right attitude and you're on the way to finding self-fulfillment in your career. Along the way you will encounter obstacles and opportunities. Sometimes the obstacles are easier to see than the opportunities. But the opportunities are there if you know where and how to look.

Seeing opportunities is only half the battle though. The important thing is to seize them. Use them. Make them work for you. It can be done.

We'll point out some of your opportunities. There are many more. Keep your eyes open and you will find them.

Employment agencies always want to send me on interviews in the least glamorous companies, in the least glamorous fields, in the least glamorous parts of town. They tell me I'm missing out on the chance of a lifetime if I refuse to go out on these job interviews. Am I?

You might be. Don't cut yourself off from any potentially exciting career opportunity. And you might not realize how exciting the opportunity is until you look into it. An opening in another industry, a nonglamorous one, could hold the possibility of getting experience you need to move ahead. Doesn't it make sense to explore this option?

Try a couple of these interviews. You can always refuse the job offer. Meanwhile, you've gotten more interview experience, talked to more people, learned about an industry or company that you had never even considered, and had one more opportunity to exercise your critical judgment. But interviews are not useful simply for the experience. You may find the career-positioning job that's right for you at this point in your career. You don't have to remain at that job forever. Career advancement comes not within one job but within a total career—*your* career.

You may decide that the job does not offer enough to counter-balance the unappealing features of the company and the locale. But you can intelligently decide that only after you have explored the possibility. Don't automatically eliminate a job before finding out what it's all about.

Meat Packing May Not Be Everyone's Idea of Glamour

Gloria was an executive secretary with ten years of work experience. A high school graduate, divorced with three children aged three to ten, Gloria went to an agency specializing in placing secretaries in New York City. She asked for an executive secretary's job with a good salary and a chance to take on more than just the standard secretarial responsibilities.

Arnie Castor, owner of the agency, urged Gloria to apply for a job with the owner of a small meat packing plant in a very nonglamorous section of New York. "The salary was very good, and she could buy meat at wholesale prices—not a small bonus for a divorced woman with three growing kids," Arnie now recalls. "I had that job specification for two weeks—no one would even go to see what the job was all about. I begged them to go. 'No way!' they all said.

"Gloria was different," Arnie continues. "Meat packing didn't sound too exciting and she didn't want to be located in that part of town, but she agreed to look into it. Her interview with the owner went well. She liked him, and she liked his attitudes. He was looking for an assistant and promised to teach her about the business. She felt she could grow on the job."

And she did! Her boss loaded on the responsibility, which she loved. Meat packing wasn't glamorous, but she was a lot closer to the actual operation of the business, and more involved in problem-solving and decision-making, than if she had been a secretary in a large, glamorous company—where her job would probably have been narrow and nonglamorous.

With outstanding communication skills, an excellent head for math, and fine follow-through, Gloria gradually started taking over most of the paper work and telephone coordination for all the buying and selling. Because of rapid fluctuations in meat prices, Gloria's careful planning and coordination were essential to company profits.

Her boss noticed her outstanding performance and rewarded her with a raise and more responsibility. Within a year and a half, Gloria was promoted to assistant buyer and authorized to hire a clerical assistant.

Her boss continued to train her to buy and sell meat. After another two and a half years, Gloria was given the official title of meat buyer and seller. She now earns fifty thousand dollars a year and hasn't typed a letter for someone else in two years.

I've heard that it's important to have a mentor if you want to move up in an organization. What does a mentor do and how would I go about finding one?

Mentors are important in the careers of many, perhaps most, successful people. Mentors have the career experience and knowledge of the company that you need to get ahead. In other words, mentors can show you the ropes. They can tell you who's who and what's what in the company. They can help you understand the real corporate structure, not just the formal organizational chart but the informal one, the one that identifies the makers and shakers in the company. By singing your praises, they can make you known to the real company leaders. They can tell you what to do and, just as important, what not to do. They can help you set priorities. They have information you can't learn in school or in books, information vital to career advancement, especially the fast-track career. You can learn it on your own, but only after years of experience. Mentors speed up your learning process by helping you avoid the mistakes *they* made.

"Great!" you may be saying at this point. "Sounds like everyone needs a mentor. Just tell me how to get one."

Acquiring a mentor is a subtle process. The mentor will choose you, not the other way around. The mentor singles you out as a person eager to learn what he or she can teach. The mentor has also found that you are enjoyable to talk to and that it is a pleasure to help you. In other words, the mentor likes you early on—enjoys being with you and seeing you develop.

Your rewards are the lessons you learn from the mentor. The mentor's rewards are the pleasures of helping to mold you and of seeing you grow professionally. But there is more. In helping to develop your values and to shape your performance, the mentor has acquired in you a potentially valuable ally with compatible attitudes toward the company and toward the job.

But you, too, have your part to play in acquiring a mentor. For one thing, you must be sensitive to a mentor's willingness to "adopt" you. For another, you must nurture the process. Send out

signals that you appreciate the advice and want more of it. Show that
you are eager to learn from the mentor. Ask questions. Following the
mentor's advice is the most visible sign of appreciation, but don't be
shy about expressing your appreciation for the mentor's help. State
your gratitude openly, plainly, and fully. Make it a pleasure to help
you.

Mentors are important in career advancement. You have much
to learn, and they can teach you. If you are open to the lessons, the
pace of your career development will quicken and each step ahead
will be more sure-footed.

The Joy of Helping and Being Helped

Karen was a graduate of a two-year junior college and of the
prestigious Katharine Gibbs secretarial school. After a brief stint as a
secretary at AT&T, she got a secretarial job at a major national news
magazine, where she worked very hard and developed a fine reputation for her competence and intelligence. She let everyone know she
was ambitious and eager to learn but did not communicate the
message in a threatening "I'm-out-to-get-your-job" manner. She
asked job-related questions of many people, but the public relations
director, Paula, seemed particularly willing to offer much-needed
advice on how to succeed at the company. She introduced Karen to
influential people, she sang her praises to them, she counseled and
supported her, and gave her feedback on her job performance and
reputation within the company. In short, Paula helped to develop
Karen's political savvy, a key ingredient in career advancement.

Thanks to Paula's advice as well as to her own developing sense
of who was doing what and where within the company, she learned
which were the best departments and most supportive bosses. And
she didn't get passed over when openings developed. After three
years at the company and numerous promotions within the
secretarial track (she worked for thirteen different people during this
period), she decided no further advancement possibilities existed
there and accepted a job as secretary to a U.S. senator.

She had been with the senator for a year when she got an excited call from Paula announcing an opening for executive secretary
to the company president. "The spot is just right for you," Paula
advised. "You should apply for it. Let me mention you for the job."
She set up an appointment between Karen and the president and,
aided by Paula's glowing recommendation, Karen got the job. Back
at the old company on her new job, Karen continued to get advice
assistance from Paula. After three more years, Karen wanted to
move out of the secretarial profession. Here again Paula was of key

importance, telling Karen how highly she was regarded by the president and advising her to seek his help in moving into another career track at the company.

At first fearful of how her boss would react, Karen finally accepted Paula's advice and decided now was the time to take a crack at getting into sales, an area she had long been interested in. Her boss created a special "cub" position for her in the sales promotion department, where she worked for four months and picked up her initial training. Then a friend alerted her to an opening as sales promotion assistant at another news magazine. She applied for the job and got it, a move approved of and applauded by her old mentor Paula.

Is job-hopping harmful to career development? Not any more. Job-hopping used to be frowned upon, at least according to conventional wisdom. Today, however, job-hopping is a standard form of career advancement at all levels of an organization. It can be a good tactic for the secretary as well as for the middle manager. If you've gone as far as you can in one organization, or if further advancement is likely to be very slow, take your skills to another employer—and perhaps upgrade your title or your job responsibilities.

Choose jobs that move you further along the path toward your career objective. Look for companies that will see beyond the secretarial label and allow you to transfer your problem-solving, decision-making, communications, people handling, and coordination skills to a nonsecretarial job. Look for companies that will add administrative responsibility and authority to your secretarial position—and, of course, a salary increase commensurate with your boost in responsibility.

Lateral moves, too, play a role in an effective job-hopping strategy. Simply changing companies, gaining new experience with a new boss, can get you out of a dead-end secretarial rut. Look for the boss who will help further your career goals. Look for the company where you can get the training and experience to move you along. Look for a company with a strong internal placement policy.

But be savvy about the job-hopping tactic. Don't use it simply to run away from problems on the job. If you've lost the focus of your job and find yourself spending too much time on menial or routine tasks, have lost sight of priorities, or resent being the one to do "housekeeping" chores (like making the coffee), you should try to resolve these problems before moving on. If your efforts fail, of course, then it's time to switch companies.

Furthermore, don't use job-hopping as a way to avoid career planning. "Job-hopping may simply indicate career immaturity," says Albert Foderaro, assistant director of career planning and placement at a New Jersey college, "Always be ready to explain to yourself and to potential employers why you made these moves."

Is there better opportunity for a secretary in a large company or a small one?

The truth is, each has its own advantages and disadvantages. It really depends on the company; size is not the determining factor. Working for the right boss is often more important.

Some of the advantages a large firm may offer include:

Education and training opportunities
Job posting
More internal placement opportunities
Regular performance appraisal system
Systematic salary review
More advanced office technology
Better benefits
Prestige and glamour
Greater chance to gain expertise in particular areas

The advantages of working for a small firm can be:

Flexibility of procedures
Variety of assignments
Visibility and a quicker road up
Less red tape
Access to key people
Fewer employees; less competition

Of course, advantages are of little value unless you take advantage of them. And this depends on your goals and your drive. A tuition refund system offered at a big organization means very little to a secretary who has no intention of furthering her education. And fewer employees in a small organization is not of much use to the secretary who wants to manage and coordinate large, diverse groups of people.

Moreover, disadvantages may often cancel out advantages. For example, competition for promotion may be less keen at smaller companies where there are fewer employees; however, because the company is small, there will be fewer openings. Or, there may be a more extensive internal placement program in a large company; however, employees may be locked into narrow categories that create overwhelming obstacles when they try to switch out of the secretarial track. Large companies do tend toward clearly defined, and possibly rigid, job classifications.

Generalizations about the advantages and disadvantages of working for a large company versus a small one can be misleading. Each company must be analyzed for its own merits and demerits. And much depends on your ability to create your own advantages or to make maximum use of existing ones.

Is it a good idea to hook up with brand new companies? Friends have warned me that you have to work ten times as hard—with no guarantees that the company will survive or that you will grow with the firm.

Start-up companies offer all of the advantages and disadvantages of working for a small company. But they offer additional benefits as well. If the company takes off, your career can take off with it. The risks may be greater, but the payoff is also greater.

Arnie Castor, the secretarial-agency owner, states categorically that "Anytime you get a chance to work at a brand-new company, grab it!" But play it smart. Job categories, company policies, and the lines of authority and responsibility have not yet had time to rigidify at start-up organizations. Take advantage of this extreme flexibility.

Make it your business to understand the objectives of the company—and then figure out ways that you can help advance these objectives. There is no better environment in which to help solve problems—these organizations have so many problems that they need everyone's input to reach solutions. As secretary, you will be at the hub of the office activities. Figure out how to coordinate procedures, assign work, improve relations with clients or customers. Get the feel of the place. Help to get it running smoothly.

When you interview for a job at a start-up organization, follow the procedures we recommended for interviewing a prospective boss. Let your boss know that you want to get ahead and will work hard to help get the company off the ground if there is growth potential for your career. Tell your boss your career objectives and ask how the company can help you advance toward them. If you are satisfied with the answer, if you're getting good vibes about the match between you and the company, go with it.

But don't forget to review your progress periodically. Chances are you will be swamped with work. But don't let a heavy work load overwhelm your sound judgment. Are you getting the type of experience you want and need? Or are you stuck with all of the routine tasks, with no time for the more challenging, career-enhancing functions? Are you satisfied with your peers' and superiors' attitudes toward you? These are the types of questions you must ask yourself at least once a month—either on the job or off. If the answers are positive, you're in the right place. If they're not, try to redesign the job to fit your needs. If your boss is not responsive to your job change suggestions, or complaints, that's not the company for you. It's time to move on!

New Firms, New Beginnings

Upon graduating from high school, Cathy accepted a position as junior secretary in a manufacturing company. She was promoted several times, advancing to executive secretary to the vice president of marketing within five years. By this time Cathy had developed superb secretarial skills and showed particular talent for dealing with people and solving problems.

After determining that this firm offered her no further growth opportunity, Cathy accepted a job at a start-up company, a radio station just purchased by new owners. Hired as one of the two secretaries in the administrative department, she handled accounts receivable and payable in addition to general secretarial duties.

She showed great initiative, ability to learn quickly, and willingness to work long hours. At the end of the year she was promoted to office manager and began hiring and supervising a growing support staff. The company continued to grow as it acquired more stations. Cathy's responsibilities grew, too. No longer tied to one office, she began training personnel at all company locations. She also helped the company to automate.

After three years, Cathy was promoted to director of administration. The following year she was given the title vice president of administration. Cathy's salary had almost tripled in three and a half years. She also had a company car. The status and rewards that Cathy had been able to achieve at this small, rapidly-growing broadcast company had exceeded her wildest dreams—but not her abilities!

I can see where new companies can offer secretaries exciting growth opportunities. But what about existing companies that are in trouble, that are cutting back expenditures and reducing staff. Should a secretary automatically get out because she cannot expect career-growth opportunities at a company fighting for survival?

No. Even in these companies, the secretary can find growth opportunities. In fact, these companies may offer an ideal chance for
the secretary to get rid of the secretarial title.

The fact is, ailing companies undergoing cutbacks will be
changing organizational structure. And when structure changes,
jobs are redesigned. Middle management layers—the better paid
and the less essential ones—are often the first to go. That's when
lower-level employees, who command lower salaries, may be asked
to take on some of the responsibilities of the higher salaried people
who are laid off.

Company mergers also offer unexpected opportunity—for some
employees. In those cases, too, staff shakeout may occur, and you
can profit from the reorganization.

If you're in a situation of this sort, stick around and see what's
in it for you. This may be an ideal time to negotiate a change in job
title: you might stay on at a low salary if your title is upgraded to
assistant personnel manager or assistant buyer or budget coordinator. Get the title first; then go after the money—either at that
company or at another one where you can apply for a job with your
upgraded title.

What else can you do?

• Volunteer to take on additional responsibilities. Size up the
company needs. Where are the holes in staffing? What can you do to
help fill them? Analyze the situation, and then tell a superior where
you want to help out. Be sure to name the job function that you can
handle—either now or after a little training.

• Look beyond the narrow confines of the secretarial job. Now
is your chance to move forward. In other words, we're not suggesting that you be "a good sport" if that means only taking on
more of the most routine secretarial tasks. Don't offer to type more
letters; offer to *draft* and type them. Don't offer to take over the filing
of a clerk who was laid off; offer a new filing system that will reduce
the office's filing burden.

Now's the chance for you to show that you can think. More
than working harder, this means working smarter. And believe us,
working smarter is the way to get ahead.

Shakeouts Can Be Sweet

Twelve years ago, Jodie worked for a candy manufacturer that
was purchased by a large corporation. When the new organization
took over, Jodie now recalls, "it turned the company upside down."

Six months after being hired, Jodie was fired. Then the personnel director, who had been Jodie's immediate boss, was fired. His assistant, Jan, was given the title of personnel manager and put in charge of the department. Jan's previous responsibilities had included record-keeping and some interviewing of job applicants, as well as the standard secretarial and clerical tasks. Now, as personnel manager, she carried out the personnel procedures and systems created by the parent company. She hired her own secrertary-clerk; the two of them constituted the personnel department.

The restructuring made dollars and sense for the parent company. Jan's previous boss, the personnel director, was easily earning more than three times her salary; Jan's salary at the time of her promotion was $7,000. The restructuring was a boon for Jan: she got a new job title, a sizable raise, and valuable experience in the field she had chosen for her career.

Can secretaries negotiate for a higher salary? When is the best time?

Salary negotiation should be a standard part of your job interview. If you don't negotiate before starting the job, you may miss out on fair treatment from the very beginning. And then you will find it extremely difficult—perhaps impossible—to catch up, because each succeeding raise is based on your original salary. If you start low, you'll stay low.

We're not advising you to make exorbitant demands. You might simply price yourself out of the job. But research the subject. Learn what the job is worth on the market. Consult employment agencies and classified ads. Your best bet is to talk to other people working at similar jobs. Getting salary information, however, is notoriously difficult. Even friends may be reluctant to divulge their salaries.

Nevertheless, try to get the subject out of the closet. It's not necessary to ask point-blank, "What do you earn?" Instead, say that you are looking for a job and want to get a better idea of what the going salaries are at your level and higher up. Ask for suggestions about what you should request. By asking for advice about your situation, other people have a choice in their response. Many will freely mention their salaries. Others may be reluctant to mention an exact figure, but will give you a range.

When soliciting this information, be prepared to disclose your own salary: "I make $15,000 now but want to ask for more on the job interview. But I need a better idea of what others get. What would you say is the salary range for secretaries at our level?" Again, this is a nonthreatening way to encourage others to reveal their salaries—or at least share what they know about salary ranges.

After you finish your research, decide what you want to ask for.

Don't drive yourself crazy coming up with *exactly* what you are worth. There is no sure-fire way to determine this. But you can set a negotiating figure for a salary range to present in the interview with a prospective boss.

It's important to suggest a range. If you get stuck on a specific figure, it will be tougher to negotiate upward.

Name the opening figures, but set them higher than you expect to get—at least five to ten percent higher. Inflating the figure by five percent is conservative, ten percent is bold. Also, decide what is the lowest figure you will accept—but keep that to yourself.

Try to learn in advance the employer's general salary range for secretaries. If you don't know this information, you will need to get it during the interview.

Don't talk about money until you have received a firm job offer. In other words, salary negotiation takes place when the interviewing stage is over. If the interviewer brings up the subject earlier, you can say something like, "Before we talk about salary, I'd like to hear more about the job itself." Or, "I don't like to talk about salary until I've been offered a position. Right now I'd like to know more about the company and the department and exactly what my role would be."

Talking more about the job and the qualifications will enable you to stress your credentials. You will then be in a stronger position when the time comes to discuss dollars and cents. Always be sure to stress your qualifications, not your needs. You are asking for a certain figure because that is what you are worth, not because that is what you need to live comfortably. Your needs are your business; your qualifications are the company's business.

Learning to negotiate salaries takes time and experience. Get your core statements ready in advance, role-play with other people, and then plunge in. The more you practice and the more real-life negotiating experience you get, the more likely you will get the salary you want—and deserve.

Suppose you do negotiate for salary, but your prospective employer refuses to budge from an initial offer that you consider too low? If you want to accept the job despite the salary, say that you would like to have a salary review in three months—after you have proven yourself on the job. A little self-promotion will come in handy here. For example, you might say: "The salary is lower than I'm looking for, but the job responsibilities and growth potential sound good, and I don't want to miss the opportunity if at all possible. I feel so confident that you will be more than satisfied with my job performance that I'd be willing to compromise now. Could we agree to something like this: I accept the job at this salary, and then we renegotiate the money in three months—after I've demonstrated my ability on the job?"

If your boss wants you a lot, there's a good chance he will agree to your suggestion. If he's lukewarm, he may hem and haw and refuse to make a definite commitment. It's then up to you to decide if you want to accept the job at that salary, with little chance for a raise in the near future.

If you decide to accept the job offer, don't worry about having tried to negotiate for a higher salary and failed. You can always yield gracefully to the employer's salary offer. For example: ''I'll take the job. The salary is not as high as I want, but the job is exactly what I want. It fits in very well with my career objectives, and it sounds like there will be good advancement possibilities.''

Even if the employer refuses to agree to a salary review, you can still bring it up again after three or six months. By then you will have demonstrated your ability. When asking for a raise while on the job, you can stress accomplishments rather than qualifications. Cite new job duties, new skills, additional responsibilities, outstanding work. You have proven your worth. Now go after the salary that rewards it.

There are three other superb opportunities for requesting a raise after you are on the job. The first is after you have completed a special project for which you have received compliments on excellent work. A second is after you have assumed new responsibilities beyond those in your original job description. A third is if you are considering another job offer.

The last situation places you in the strongest position, for your current employer would be competing with another for your continued services. You might say something like: ''I have been offered another job at a higher salary, and am seriously considering it. I like this company and I like my job, but if I stay here I want a raise. Can you give me a raise of $—?''

Keep your eyes open for these and other opportunities to negotiate a suitable salary.

How important is a college degree for a secretary?

This is a tricky question—and the answer is not simple. One thing is obvious: educational requirements have stiffened. In the past, many secretaries were able to use natural abilities, take-charge attitudes, and on-the-job experience to advance outside of the secretarial field without a college degree. Today, in many fields, a college degree, sometimes even an advanced college degree, is obligatory.

College grads today, and throughout the 1980's, are faced with a highly competitive job market. The Bureau of Labor Statistics reports that about 15 million college graduates will enter the labor force in the 1980s; and 2 to 3 million of them won't get jobs that usually require a college degree. Moreover, these new college grads will be competing with the 3.8 million graduates in the labor force since the end of 1980 who are either in jobs not requiring a college degree or are unemployed.

Many industries today adopt the attitude that with so many unemployed college grads around, why should they hire a candidate without a degree? In such companies, advancement will not come without that piece of paper. Certainly in companies dealing in very specialized and or technical knowledge, a secretary without a degree has little chance of advancement.

Do not despair. If you have what it takes to get ahead—the drive, the focus, the awareness, the native intelligence—you have what it takes to get a B.A. or a B.S. And employers don't often ask about the quality of the school: the diploma is enough to demonstrate basic academic competence.

On the other hand, many studies show that the money and time spent on college education could earn more if invested in the real world of work and experience. If you're a lively, ambitious, sensible person, you could waste time and money getting a standard college degree. Your career might develop faster with on-the-job experience. In fact, there are still many fields where a college degree is not required. Sales is an obvious example. Even in the new information and high-technology industries, creative, entrepreneurial spirit may sometimes be more valuable that a piece of paper.

If college degrees are no guarantee for success, what is the winning educational strategy to pursue today in search of a challenging and rewarding career? We recommend *targeted education.*

This is a straightforward strategy. After identifying your career objectives, get a job with growth potential and then, while getting on-the-job experience, target your education to your career objective. This might mean getting a degree from a two-year college, a . four-year college, a technical institute, or a graduate school.

Targeted education will enable you to fill your knowledge gaps as they change—and they will change as you grow on the job—and to to meet your increased responsibilities. The world is changing and the technical knowledge required to make it in our new world is changing.

Talk to your superiors or to your personnel department. Get their advice on what education you need to do your job better and to move along your chosen career path. Then go out and get the education. You will find this to be a challenging and rewarding task, if not an easy one (especially if you hold a job at the same time). But don't worry about the difficulties of going back to school. Don't worry that

166   NOT *JUST* A SECRETARY

you may be older than most of your classmates. You have an important advantage, real work experience, which can make you a
valuable addition to your class.

Targeted education, of course, is not limited to a classroom.
Learning acquired on the job is every bit as valuable, perhaps more
so, than that acquired in school. Don't downgrade your experience—and don't let others downgrade it either.

*What job market realities lie ahead in the next decade or two? Do they really
affect me?*

Job market realities certainly do affect you. They set the
framework within which you will be starting a career, advancing in
it, and, perhaps, switching fields. Economic and job market realities
can help you, hurt you, and point you in certain directions; they are
never irrelevant. Ignoring them is a mistake, for they won't ignore
you.

These are some of the major factors that will affect your career
potential in the mid- and late-1980s.

• White-collar employees are now a majority in America, con-
stituting just over half of the working population in 1980 as opposed
to only one-third in 1950. White-collar occupations include professional, managerial, sales, and clerical jobs, with the clerical
group—your group as a secretary—the largest occupational
category.

• Employment in white-collar occupations is expected to increase between 18 and 26 percent by 1990, according to the Bureau
of Labor Statistics, creating between nine and thirteen million jobs.
Demand for managers, clerical workers, professionals, and sales
workers all will be on the rise.

• Automation is an inescapable fact of our working lives today
and will be even more so tomorrow. Don't fight it, use it! Find out
where the opportunities are. New career possibilities will open for
secretaries as a result of office automation. But computers will
eliminate many jobs, too, for they can handle routine clerical work
more quickly and efficiently than humans can.

• Companies and industries based on new electronic
technologies seem to promise the greatest growth in the coming
decades. Technical skills and knowledge will most likely be
obligatory. Find out what skills you need. Then get them.

• Americans have always been on the move, going to new
regions in search of opportunity. Today is no exception. The shift in
recent years has been to the South and the West, and away from the

Northeast and Midwest. Just three states—California, Texas, and Florida—together account for more than 20 percent of the jobs in the U.S. and have experienced the greatest growth in population. However, be aware that patterns shift; moreover, you may simply not fit the pattern and can find your career-positioning job in a "dying" region as well as a growing one. Many factors must be taken into account, and regional growth is only one.

Change is threatening to some, but it is always an opportunity for those with the courage to grab the new. Be ready to spot the opportunities—and go after them.

Chapter Sixteen

Putting It Together
to Get Ahead

"Oh, it just happened. . . . "
"I was in the right place at the right time. . . ."
"The luck of the Irish . . . only I'm not Irish. . . ."

All of these time-worn sayings help to explain Sarah Martin's career path from secretary to associate administrator of City of Hope Medical Center without benefit of a college degree. But the real key, she believes, is attitude.

Sarah sees herself as:

• A risk taker—"Although I feel rather timid in that area, I realize I have been bold," she says. "Perhaps it's the 'where angels fear to tread' syndrome. Today you might call it assertiveness, which is especially important for women in what often is still a man's world."

• A doer—"more apt to just get on with getting things done than waiting for someone else to do it or think of it."

• A high-energy, active person—"I'm always into something, going places, arranging things. I like to stay busy."

Sarah enjoys other winning traits as well. She displays the confidence that comes from an I-can-do attitude; she has a lively sense of curiosity and constantly asks what makes something tick, how does it work, what if it were this way. She is challenged by difficulty and fascinated by people. She loves to help people find better ways to do things. "All of these things gave me the wherewithal to turn a secretarial job into an exciting, rewarding career," Sarah concludes.

Sarah's upward climb was not easy, nor was it easy for the other secretaries who told us how they got ahead in their careers. But getting ahead is never easy. It takes hard work, it takes willingness to make mistakes (and to learn from those mistakes), it takes a desire to grow and to realize one's fullest potential—and it takes courage.

Change requires courage. The old ways are secure. The secretary and her boss are settled into familiar patterns with which each feels comfortable. The boss generally offers guidance and protection. Giving up the security blanket is not easy.

Learning from failure also takes courage. We all know that no one is perfect. But somehow it's hard to really accept that fact of life—especially when it applies to us. No one likes to make mistakes, but everyone does. Accepting the fact that you will make mistakes as you chart new waters and take on expanded responsibility is not easy. While it's possible to be letter-perfect when typing a letter, there really is no such thing as a "perfect" decision or a "perfect"solution to a problem. The idea of perfection in such situations is, frankly, irrelevant. It just doesn't apply. You can make good, even excellent, decisions, but necessary compromise and less-than-perfect conditions will make any decision less than "perfect."

Courage is required to overcome the fear of success, too. But, you may be thinking, we just said that you may be afraid to fail. Are we now saying that you may also be afraid to succeed? Yes! Research in recent years, particularly by Mattina Horner, psychologist and president of Radcliffe College, suggests that many women are afraid of success because they are afraid of possible negative consequences, such as unpopularity and loss of femininity. Such fears sap women of their will to compete openly with men and holds them back from career advancement.

What might you give up as you move ahead in your career? The loss of your boss's protection and praise. An end to the 9-to-5 work day. And more subtle losses. If you are a secretary at the highest levels of the organization, you may have no desire to switch career tracks and land a bottom-level managerial position far removed from high-level management. You may have to give up prestige, salary, drapes, and other perks that come with being near a top executive. You may have to sacrifice the excitement and challenge of being close to the top decision-makers.

Switching to the managerial track has another serious drawback: there will be times when you feel "out of your league." Sarah Martin did! Of course, adjustment is much easier if you get support from your new peers and your new superiors. But this may not be the case. Your advancement may be hard for them, too.

"Once a secretary, always a secretary" may be their attitude—and they can show it in many ways. You may still be the one to make or serve the coffee at meetings. You may take the notes at the meetings. You may be excluded from the lunches where so much business is conducted and where business and personal friendships are cemented. You may. . . well, you may get the feeling you're out of your league!

What we're saying is that when you change roles, when you assume additional responsibility and additional status, your anxiety quotient will probably rise at first. That is normal. But you can overcome this anxiety. Perhaps the best way is not to hide your secretarial origins but just the opposite. Make full and openly obvious use of the many skills that made you a successful secretary. Many of those skills, as we've said again and again in this book, are precisely the skills you need to succeed at the higher levels of an organization.

What about those peers and superiors who try to keep you in your place? It's up to you to let them know how natural it is for you to adapt to a new "place." They may be carrying around society's old patronizing attitude toward the secretary. It's not easy to shuck this attitude. It may not have been easy for you, and it will probably be even harder for others.

Don't forget that some of your new higher-level peers may actually resent your advancement. They may feel threatened by it. They may see you as competition for the limited number of growth positions on the career ladder. In short, they may have their own career anxieties.

How to cope? By remembering your secretarial origins. Don't deny them. But don't deny your ambition either. Use your secretarial skills to add to your effectiveness in the new position. For example, what about keeping the minutes at a meeting? Is this a low-status chore? Or, can it be a challenging communication function that makes the difference between productive and unproductive meetings?

There's nothing routine about taking good notes at a meeting. Consider the experience of Jim, who joined Myrna's company as controller and within four months was vice president of finance and administration. Jim took notes at meetings—very good notes. After meetings he would circulate a memo that summarized what had been decided at the meeting, what follow-up was required, and who was responsible for the follow-ups. Now, obviously, Jim's rapid advancement within the organization could not be ascribed simply to his taking notes at meetings. But his memos were one of the tools he used to increase his value to the organization.

You can act likewise. Look for ways to transform routine chores into valuable functions. There's no reason, for example, why you could not send similar post-meeting memos recapitulating the decisions and then adding your own suggestions for how to implement the decisions. If you have additional thoughts about matters discussed at the meeting, why not express them in the memo? After all, who gets all her ideas during one limited time period? Perhaps your best ideas come only after you give additional thought to a subject. If so, a memo would help you communicate these ideas to others in the organization.

In general, treat your peers as comrades and expect them to treat you the same way. In time this will become the new reality—for you and for them. But you will need patience. It's not easy to train others to change their perceptions, but that is what you are doing. You are training others to view you differently—as not just a secretary.

And what do you gain as you move ahead in your career? We've already talked about the growing pains associated with career advancement. Now let's talk about the "growing gains."

Salary. Leaving the secretarial track does not immediately translate into a higher salary. Secretaries, particularly experienced secretaries, command higher salaries than employees in many lower-level professional and managerial positions. This is one of the factors that keep many secretaries from making a career switch—no matter how much they complain about being just a secretary. Nevertheless, the potential for higher salaries is there once you gain the necessary experience in a managerial or professional position. If you choose to remain a secretary, expanding your job description to reflect additional responsibilities will carry salary increases, too, some of them quite hefty.

Independence. "You're not really in control when you're a secretary," according to Nancy Blake, who switched from being a secretary to a radio advertising salesperson. Nancy felt very restricted taking orders on a daily basis, sometimes on an hourly basis, from a boss. She yearned for freedom to set her own schedule and to meet the company goals in *her* way. She wanted freedom from a desk and from the many routine tasks required of her as a secretary.

In her new career—her chosen career—Nancy found the wider scope of action she was looking for. She makes more decisions on her own, and those decisions have direct impact on the radio station's bottom line. And, perhaps most important, Nancy accepts the consequences of independence. Indeed, she relishes them: she likes being held accountable for her decisions.

Variety. Switching career tracks or advancing within the secretarial profession brings the "fun of diversification, the adventure of new problems to solve,'' to quote Sarah Martin. And it is fun.

It is fun to encounter new challenges. It is fun to successfully meet those challenges. It is fun to learn from them. Not only is it fun, it is also enriching. We're not talking primarily about financial enrichment, although of course we have nothing against it! We're thinking more of psychological enrichment, the satisfaction that comes from thinking better of yourself because you like what you are doing and how you are doing it. With psychological enrichment comes a broader outlook, increased adaptability, and perhaps very different kinds of experience.

Variety also adds to one's portfolio of skills, which leads to growth.

Growth. The ultimate "growing gain" is the joy you gain from growth itself—growth as a serious professional in whatever career path you choose. You can feel your growth. You can see your growth. You can do things you were not able to do before. You can build on your achievements. To grow is to expand your potential. To grow is to feel alive.

You are not *just* a secretary, whether you decide to stay in the secretarial profession or to use it as a stepping-stone to another career. You can be an important member of whatever organization you work for. You *are* an important member if you choose to be one. You are important if you see yourself as important. And seeing yourself as important is the surest way to get others to see you the same way. It can be done. *You* can do it!

Recommended Reading

Bloom, Lynn Z., Karen Cobun, and Joan Pearlman. *The New Assertive Woman*. New York: Delacorte Press, 1981.
A how-to manual useful for strengthening your image and your
ability to deal with conflict.

Bolles, Richard N. *What Color Is Your Parachute?* Berkeley, Calif.:
Ten   Speed Press, 1982.
Describes the less traditional methods for career search, with
strong emphasis on identifying your most important skills.
Excellent book to have in your library.

Catalyst Staff. *Marketing Yourself: The Catalyst Women's Guide to Successful Resumes and Interviews*. New York: G. P. Putnam's Sons,
1980.
Excellent advice for resume writing and interviewing for a job.

Catalyst Staff. *Upward Mobility*. New York: Holt, Rinehart & Winston,
1982.
Good all-around resource book. Chapter 9, "Hitch a Rise on A
Coattail!" deals with mentors and networking—and how to find a
network for you.

Chastain, Sherry. *Winning the Salary Game: Salary Negotiation for
Women*. New York: John Wiley & Sons, Inc., 1980.
Everything you need to know about negotiating salary, including
the best negotiating outfit (p. 117).

Figler, Howard. *The Complete Job-Search Handbook*. New York: Holt,
Rinihart & Winston, 1979.
One of our career-planning favorites. If you are in need of a
good pick-me-up, we recommend chapter 25, "Zen of the
Work Search."

Harragan, Betty Lehan. *Games Mother Never Taught You: Corporate
Gamesmanship for Women*. New York: Warner Books, 1980.
If you think you need "toughening up" in corporate politics, this
book should do it for you. We particularly recommend chapter 9,
"The Bottom Line—Money," if you need help in asking for a
raise.

Irish, Richard K. *If Things Don't Improve Soon, I May Ask You to Fire Me: The Management Book for Everyone Who Works*. Garden City, New York: Anchor Press, Doubleday, 1976.
Down-to-earth information for both employers and employees. We particularly recommend chapter 4 on growth jobs and chapter 5 on resumes.

Jackson, Tom. *The Perfect Resume*. Garden City, New York: Anchor Press, Doubleday, 1981.
An excellent guide to writing resumes and cover letters.

Kandler Thelma. *What Women Earn*. New York: The Linden Press, Simon and Schuster, 1981.
Lists dozens of occupations, their growth potential, and salary information. Pages 43–49 deal with secretaries. We highly recommend this book for help in exploring the job market.

Kantor, Rosabeth Moss. *Men and Women of the Corporation*. New York: Basic Books, Inc., 1977.
Analyzes the corporate structure and how it affects the career and self-image of the secretary (pp.69–104).

Malloy, John. *Dress for Success*. New York: Follett, 1977.
Pages 124 and 125 offer tips for the secretary, but read the whole book for Malloy's overall clothing advice to upwardly mobile women.

Smith, Manuel J. *When I Say No, I Feel Guilty*. New York: Dial Press, 1975.
Gives excellent assertive techniques for coping with criticism, avoiding manipulation, and developing persistence.

Taetzch, Lyn, and Eileen Benson. *Taking Charge on the Job: Techniques for Assertive Management*. New York: Ballantine Books, 1978.
We highly recommend this book for aid in developing assertive communication skills on the job.

Working Woman Magazine. *The Working Woman Success Book*. New York: Ace Books, 1981.
Many articles written by experts in the field. We particularly recommend the section on asking for a raise.

Periodicals

Many monthly publications with excellent articles on the working woman are available at the newsstands. Those we consider consistently helpful are: *Ms.*, *Savvy*, and *Working Woman*. In addition, *The Secretary*, is published nine times a year by the Professional Secretaries International (see appendix). It is available to members only.

Three free, specialized magazines are geared to beginners in office automation. They are available by writing to the magazines.

Modern Office Procedures
P.O. Box 91368
Cleveland, OH   44101

The Office
Office Publications, Inc.
P.O. Box 13205
Philadelphia, PA   19101

Today's Office
P.O. Box 619
Garden City, NY   11530

An excellent magazine for more in-depth, higher-level information on office automation is available through paid subscription:

Office Administration and Automation
Geyer–McAllister Publications, Inc.
51 Madison Avenue
New York, NY   10010

Networks and Professional Associations

There are many networks and associations that can be important sources for information, job leads, advice, and contacts. Share names and experiences with your friends and acquaintances. Get other names of organizations from your local *Yellow Pages*, under "Associations," according to the fields of your choice. Ask your librarian for books that list associations, and choose the appropriate ones for you. If the organization is in your city, arrange a meeting with a staff member to learn what it offers. If it is not near you, write for brochures and other information.

The following associations are worth a visit or a letter.

Catalyst
14 East 60th Street
New York, NY   10022
(212) 759-9700

The Catalyst Network describes itself as a "group of independent resource centers that provide career and educational guidance for women. . . .Centers affiliated with the Catalyst Network must meet criteria established by Catalyst to ensure that they conform to professional standards. Catalyst centers provide career services for women who wish to advance their careers, change fields, or reenter the job market." For information on the center closest to you, contact the main office listed above.

Professional Secretaries International
2440 Pershing Road
Kansas City, MO   64108
(816) 474-5755

Professional Secretaries International, originally known as the National Secretaries Association, was the first of the Secretarial Networks founded in 1942. PSI, as it is commonly known, offers members a variety of workshops and forums devoted to the secretary's professional development. A nominal membership fee entitles members to copies of *The Secretary*, an outstanding publication that is chockfull of information dealing with such topics as compensation, career development, automation, sexual harassment, and other important issues. PSI recognizes the importance of distinguishing between those who look upon secretarial work as a career and those who are interested in the job as a springboard to another field. It addresses the needs of both groups.

Certified Professional Secretary Certification (CPS) PSI sponsors certification to secretaries who complete satisfactorily a two-day examination based on office procedures, business skills, economics, management, and behavioral science. Earning the certification identifies the secretary as exceptional according to measurable standards.

The examination is given in May in 250 different locations. Applicants must file on or before December 1.

To get an application and information about the exam, write to:

Certified Professional Secretary
Professional Secretaries International
2440 Pershing Road
Kansas City, MO   64108

Office Automation Word and Office Automation information processing continues to grow, and the number of professional associations you can join continues to grow, too. For a start, you may want to contact:

International Word Processing Association
   Headquarters
   1015 N. York Road
   Willow Grove, PA   19090
   (215) 657-3220
      For information write: Linda O'Keeffe, president

International Association of Word Processing Specialists
   1669 S. Voss, Suite 100
   Houston, TX   77057
   (713) 820-8555
      For information write: Jeff James, director of membership

Index

listening and, 93
with a prospective boss, 129–140
salary negotiations, 139, 162–164
tips for asking questions, 134

Job clarifying questions, 136–137
Job-hopping, 157–158
Job information:
  contacts, 89–90
  interviews, 91–94
  library research, 85–89
  source books for, 85–88
Job market, future and, 166–167
Job posting system, 128, 137

Library, career planning use of, 85–89
Listening effectively, 39–43
  active techniques, 40–42
  interviews and, 93
  passive techniques, 40
  pointers for, 42–43
Long term goals, 99

Manipulative criticism, 53–60
  See also Criticism.
Masochism, criticism and, 54
Memos:
  use in confrontation, 73–76
  writing tips, 75
Mentors, 155–156

Networks:
  interviews, 91–94
  making contacts, 89–90
Nonverbal behavior, image and, 26–28

Occupational Outlook Handbook, 85, 86–87
Office games, 45–51
  authority conflicts, 45–47
  avoiding dependence, 60–63
  claiming due credit, 63–65
  evaluation of conflict
    situations, 48–49
  manipulative criticism, 53–60

redefinition of conflict
  situations, 49–51
  taking charge, 65–68
Office procedure, 16
Organizational restructuring:
  automation and, 144
  career advancement and, 161–162

Passive listening, 40
Personnel department, within-company
  advancement and, 126–128
Problem solving, 15
Public relations, 13–14

Quitting, criticism and, 59–60

Reference books, job research and, 88
Research, use of library, 85–89
Resumes, 103–110
  basic rules for, 104
  chronological resume, 106–107
  chronological resume, sample, 111
  functional resume, 107–110
  functional resume, sample, 112
  ongoing updates of, 110
  organization of, 104–105
  tips for preparation of, 109–110

Salary gains, career advancement
  and, 172
Salary negotiation, 139, 162–164
Satisfaction, career advancement
  and, 172
Secretaries:
  career decisions, 95–101
  career planning, 77–82
  college degree and, 164–166
  job market for, 6
  role appreciation and, 9–10
  short/long/intermediate
    goals, 98–100
  steps toward advancement, 4, 6
  targeted education, 165–166
  techniques to begin a career, 6–7
Self-respect, criticism and, 54